Martin Buber's
I and Thou

Practicing Living Dialogue

Martin Buber's
I and Thou

Practicing Living Dialogue

I am no prophet, philosopher, or theologian.
I am simply a man who has seen something and
who goes to the window and points to what he sees.
—MARTIN BUBER

KENNETH PAUL KRAMER
WITH MECHTHILD GAWLICK

PAULIST PRESS
New York/Mahwah, N.J.

Cover design by Sharyn Banks
Book design by Sharyn Banks and Theresa M. Sparacio

Library of Congress Cataloging-in-Publication Data

Kramer, Kenneth, 1941–
    Martin Buber's I and Thou : practicing living dialogue / Kenneth Paul Kramer with Mechthild Gawlick.
        p. cm.
"I am no prophet, philosopher, or theologian. I am simply a man who has seen something and who goes to the window and points to what he sees—Martin Buber." Includes bibliographical references and index.
    ISBN 0-8091-4158-2 (alk. paper)
    1. Buber, Martin, 1878-1965. Ich und du. 2. Life. 3. Relationism.
I. Gawlick, Mechthild. II. Title.
B3213.B83I2355 2003
299′.51482—dc21

                                      2003013705

Published by Paulist Press
997 Macarthur Boulevard
Mahwah, New Jersey 07430

www.paulistpress.com

Printed and bound in the United States of America

Contents

Contents

To the "anonymous donor"
whose gift to one becomes a blessing for all

That peoples can no longer carry on authentic dialogue with one another is not only the most acute symptom of the pathology of our time, it is also that which most urgently makes a demand of us. I believe, despite all, that the peoples in this hour can enter into dialogue, into a genuine dialogue with one another. In a genuine dialogue each of the partners, even when he stands in opposition to the other, heeds, affirms, and confirms his opponent as an existing other. Only so can conflict certainly not be eliminated from the world, but be humanly arbitrated and led towards its overcoming.

—MARTIN BUBER
"Genuine Dialogue and the Possibilities of Peace"

Foreword

MAURICE FRIEDMAN

Many years ago I gave a lecture for a group of Labor Zionists in New York City. During the question period the woman who had arranged for me to come there asked me, "Why is it that *dialogue* and *commitment* are such popular words today?" "I suppose because there is so little of either!" I replied. I imagine almost everyone by now has heard of Martin Buber's central term *dialogue,* though few probably understand it in the depth that Buber did. After Buber's death his great disciple, the Israeli educator Ernst Simon, commented that the life of dialogue to which Buber pointed will probably remain part of our heritage after Buber himself is forgotten.

Less than a year ago, newspapers in many parts of America carried the story of an anonymous donor who gave a remarkably generous monetary grant to Professor Kenneth Kramer of the Comparative Religious Studies Program at San José State University in order that he might take a year off and write a popular book that would bring Martin Buber to a far larger audience than he has ever reached. The result is Kenneth Kramer's remarkable book *Martin Buber's* I and Thou: *Practicing Living Dialogue.*

I can think of no work of more lasting importance for our times than Martin Buber's *I and Thou.* During more than half a century of work on Martin Buber's life and work, including fifteen years of close interchange with Martin Buber himself in connection with my translation of a dozen of his writings from German into English, his three trips to America, and my own stay in Jerusalem in 1960, my conviction has been steadily strengthened that *I and Thou* has a saving message for our time. In my three-volume study *Martin Buber's Life and Work* and my one-volume *Encounter on the Narrow Ridge: A Life of Martin Buber,* I have depicted Buber's road to *I and Thou* and have shown how much of his later thought and action has grown out of it.

Dag Hammarskjöld, the great secretary general of the United Nations, was translating *I and Thou* into Swedish at the time that his plane was tragically shot down in the Congo. *I and Thou* has been translated into a great many languages, and numerous commentaries have been written on it, including one that recasts it in the language of linguistic analytical philosophy. What Nietzsche's *Thus Spoke Zarathustra* was to the nineteenth century, Buber's *I and Thou* has been to the twentieth, and to us who live in the twenty-first century too.

Buber wrote *I and Thou* in a sort of ecstasy in which he did not choose a language but "what was to be said formed it as the tree its bark." For this very reason Buber said many years later that he could not risk changing the text because there was no way to know what might be lost in so doing. There is indeed a unique fusion of content and poetic language in *I and Thou* that makes it as difficult to paraphrase as it is to paraphrase a true poem.

Despite this, Kenneth Kramer's book has provided a unique service for *I and Thou* as none of the other commentaries have done. He has managed to get into its heart; to choose its central themes; to illustrate them by quotation, interpretation, diagram, and reference to other of Buber's works; and to put them into language that makes Buber's thought accessible to a great many people who might otherwise find it impossible to grasp. I am particularly delighted with the two chapters with which Kramer concludes this book: "The Way of 'Turning'" and "The Way of 'Inclusion.'" Indeed, Professor Kramer has performed his service so well that I would not hesitate to urge the publishers of *I and Thou* to bring out Kramer's *Martin Buber's* I and Thou as a companion piece to the original.

Since by far the largest number of readers of Kramer's book do not have access to the German original of *I and Thou,* another service that Kenneth Kramer has performed is to list in parallel columns key passages from the two English translations of *I and Thou* (Ronald Gregor Smith [1958]; Walter Kaufmann [1970]), as well as occasionally selecting one or the other translation of a given passage as superior to the other. Occasionally, moreover, he and his dialogical partner—the German-speaking Mechthild Gawlick—have offered translations of their own that they think better than either Smith or Kaufmann. Professor Kramer has dealt with these translations fairly and even-handedly, which is a good thing not only in itself, but also because the publishers of *I and Thou,* despite promises to keep both translations in print, have retained the Smith one only as a rather expensive Scribner's Classic. Still, I must confess that for me the Ronald Gregor Smith translation is by far superior to the later one by Kaufmann. Martin Buber himself worked with Smith on this translation, while Kaufmann's translation was authorized by Buber's son Raphael after Buber's death.

I can only wish this book well and hope it reaches the wide audience that it deserves and for whom it can have great meaning. As Buber himself said at the end of his 1958 "Postscript" to *I and Thou,* in bearing witness he also "calls to witness him to whom he speaks—whether that witness be now or in the future."

Acknowledgments

Martin Buber's I and Thou has been a work in progress for several years and continues to unfold through the ongoing interactions that it engenders. Many people have contributed ideas, insights, and encouragement to this project, including family, friends, students, and colleagues. Specifically, I am especially grateful to Maurice Friedman, who introduced me to the profound significance of Martin Buber's writings and who helped me fine tune the book. As well, I am grateful to Michael Sing, Leila Kramer, Dieter Gawlick, Will McKinley, Mishael Caspi, James Franks, and particularly to James Brown, all of whom provided invaluable feedback and cogent suggestions in response to preliminary versions of the manuscript, and to the copyeditor, Joan Laflamme, for impeccable attention to the details. Also, I wish to thank Noah Klocek for the graphics in Chapters 2, 3, 5, and 6, and certainly my tireless typist, Jeffrey Strafford.

Most significantly, I want to thank Mechthild Gawlick, my dialogical partner, who has been fully present at every step along the way. Her double cultural context, astute translations, and her life of "living dialogue" embody and express a deep understanding of Buber's *I and Thou*. This book would not have come to fruition without her continued, co-creative inspiration and support.

Martin Buber

CHRONOLOGY

1878	February 8, Martin Buber born in Vienna.
1881	Mother deserts the family.
1881–1891	Following the divorce of his parents, Buber is educated by his grandparents, Solomon Buber (property owner, banker, editor of Hebrew Midrashic literature) and Adele Buber (property caretaker and reader of German classics) in Vienna.
1896	Studies philosophy at the University of Vienna and the University of Leipzig; joins a Zionist movement.
1899	Summer studies at the University of Zurich; meets and marries Paula Winkler, a writer from Munich.
1900–1901	Births of Rafael (1900) and Eva (1901).
1904	Completes doctoral dissertation on German Mysticism at the University of Vienna.

Toward *I and Thou*

1906	Settles in Berlin for ten years.
1907–1908	Publishes Hasidic books—*Tales of Rabbi Nachman* and *Legend of Baal-Shem*—written in Italy.
1910	Publishes *Speeches and Allegories of Chuang-Tzu,* along with an Afterword, "The Teaching of the Tao."
1913	Publishes *Daniel*—first use of "inclusion" *(Umfassung).*
1914	Buber's "conversion" event.

Martin Buber's *I and Thou*

1916	First brief sketch of *I and Thou*.
1919	First rough draft of *I and Thou*.
1921–1922	Beginnings of closer relationship with Franz Rosenzweig; lecture series (January-March 1922) "Religion as Presence."
1923	Publishes *I and Thou (Ich und Du)*.

Frankfurt Years

1923	Appointed professor of Jewish history of religion and ethics, Frankfurt University.
1925	Begins translation of Hebrew Bible into German with Franz Rosenzweig.
1930	Promoted to professorship at the University of Frankfurt.
1935	Invited to Hebrew University, Jerusalem.

Jerusalem Years

1938	Leaves Germany in March; professorship of social philosophy at Hebrew University, Jerusalem. Later, first chairman of new Department of Sociology.
1948	Publishes *Between Man and Man*.
1951–1952	Lecture tour in the United States.
1953	Awarded Peace Prize of the German Book Trade; "Genuine Dialogue and the Possibilities of Peace."
1957	Meets Carl Rogers at the University of Michigan; writes "Postscript" for new edition of *I and Thou*.
1958	Paula Buber dies in Venice.
1960	Publishes *Meetings* (autobiographical fragments).
1963	Receives the Erasmus Award in Amsterdam.
1965	Publishes *The Knowledge of Man*; June 13, Buber dies at home in Talbiyeh, Jerusalem.

Introduction
GENUINE DIALOGUE

> There is something that can only be found in one
> place. It is a great treasure, which may be called the
> fulfillment of existence. The place where this treasure
> can be found is the place on which one stands.
> —MARTIN BUBER, *The Way of Man*

Whether descriptive of a failed marriage or collapsed peace
negotiations, confusion, disagreement, and misunderstanding,
usually called communication breakdown, often thwart human
relationships at every level. Beneath the chaos of warring monologues, though, two dimensions of human interaction have continued to receive widespread attention across a spectrum of fields
and social situations. The first is the feeling almost everybody has
that meaningful communication is absolutely necessary to the survival of individuals and nations. This dimension is mitigated by a
second, the daunting understanding that such communication is
difficult, and usually seems impossible, to attain.

Of many possible responses to this difficult situation, our
central interest in this book focuses on Martin Buber's liberating
alternative: the life of "genuine dialogue." To articulate Buber's
understanding of engaged interaction, we will simplify and clarify
the core teachings of Buber's classic, *I and Thou*. This book,
accordingly, has a double intention. First, it is meant to accent the
central address of Buber's 1923 masterpiece by rephrasing and
discussing its three main parts. Parallel to this, in the process of

looking at the layers of meaning in *I and Thou,* we will set out to clarify and accent Buber's leading dialogical principles in order to challenge and improve the quality of private and public discourse, especially about moral conflicts. To begin, we must understand that barriers to meaningful communication are multiple, and manifest everywhere.

From Debate to Dialogue

Professor C. David Mortensen, in *Miscommunication* (1992), offers a long list of obstacles to dialogue that includes withholding, expectations, biases, deceptions, disruptions, conflicts, ambiguities, and vagueness. Of primary concern for Mortensen is the composite impact of faulty assumptions, inferences, and expectations about the possibility of communicating clearly and effectively. As diverging viewpoints between communicants in any conversation increase, the need to develop communication-supportive resources becomes more acute.

A few years later, along similar lines, Professor Deborah Tannen, in *The Argument Culture* (1998), approaches the problem less theoretically. She proposes that mentalities of debate and criticism shape our turn-of-the-century culture of thought. She suggests that communication in the "argument culture" (which means approaching people in an adversarial frame of mind) encourages people to distort facts, to polarize views, to waste time, and to limit thinking. According to Tannen, the argument culture pervades every aspect of our social lives from global warming to abortion.

To overcome the knee-jerk "American habit" of depicting issues as two-sided dialectical arguments, Tannen points out the need to find metaphors other than "sports and war" to describe human interactions. Even more significantly, she indicates that we must expand our notion of debate to include dialogue. One of the consequences of what she calls the "debate culture" (a shared need to be right, to look good, to win, to convince, to prove, to judge, to rebut, to justify, to defend) is the tendency to equate intelligence with the ability to argue well. In place of the practice of spontaneous monologues, she suggests, we need to build a "dialogue culture"; our very public and private lives are at stake. Toward this goal she proposes alternative ways of speaking:

INSTEAD OF THIS...	SAY THIS...
Battle of the sexes	Relations between women and men
Debate	Discuss
War on drugs	Solving the drug problem
Focus on differences	Search for common ground
The opposition party	The other party
The argument culture	The dialogue culture

What Mortensen's and Tannen's books have in common is fairly basic: They both point out that it is imperative to engage in and support the emergence of a dialogical culture, both in our interpersonal lives and in institutional decision-making. According to Buber, despite the progressive burial of truly human relationships, this hour's hope "depends upon the renewal of dialogical immediacy between men" *(Pointing the Way, 228)*. Engaging in genuine dialogue enhances the possibilities for meaningful community, and for realizing our unique wholeness. In this book, therefore, we will *hear* about, *ponder,* and begin to *practice* what Martin Buber calls the ever-new "dialogical relationship" that often remains "hidden in our midst." For this reason we turn to Buber's unusual perspective on human interaction in *I and Thou* with the conviction, based on our shared experiences, that practicing Buberian dialogue brings attitude-changing results to human relationships.

Martin Buber (1878–1965)

The transforming possibilities of "genuine dialogue" were first signaled by the renowned German Jewish religious and philosophical scholar, Martin Buber, in the years surrounding the first and second world wars. Born in Vienna, he studied philosophy at the universities of Vienna, Munich, and Leipzig. A man of encyclopedic knowledge—Buber was fluent in nine languages—perhaps his greatest contribution to the human community was sixty years of pointing to the hidden treasure he called the "life of dialogue."

In 1953 Buber was awarded the Peace Prize of the German Book Trade for practicing and recording just this kind of life. Fittingly, Arthur Georgi, who presented the award, characterized Buber as a true person who "fashions a humane spirit suffusing all living things." As a philosopher, poet, novelist, dramatist, and translator and interpreter of the Hebrew Bible, Buber was nominated for a Nobel Prize in literature by Herman Hesse. Little wonder, then, that when Buber died in 1965, he was eulogized as one of the greatest human beings of the twentieth century.

When looking at any historical figure, one soon becomes aware of the relation between what a person says of himself or herself as distinct from what others say. In *Philosophical Interrogations,* for instance, Buber writes: "*I must* philosophize; there is no other way to my goal, but my goal itself cannot be grasped philosophically" (17). While this is true, Buber still remained a philosopher for life, albeit an atypical one. As he said of himself in *The Philosophy of Martin Buber,* he felt duty-bound to bring "decisive experiences" into the "human inheritance of thought...as an insight valid and important for others" (689). Indeed, Buber referred to himself as "a trustworthy elaborator" who was committed to the task of explaining "attained insights" emerging from both personal experiences and interpersonal interactions.

Though he is often called a philosophical anthropologist or a religious existentialist, Buber was by his own definition a *Schriftsteller* (both a writer and one who renders scriptures). Throughout his later writings Buber strove to be one who simply pointed to the life of dialogue. Philosophy, sociology, and religion all played into his world view. Indeed, toward the end of his life Buber was asked if he was a theologian or a philosopher. In response, in *The Philosophy of Martin Buber,* he remarked:

> I must say it once again: I have no teaching. I only point to something...I point to something in reality that had not or had too little been seen. I take him who listens to me by the

4

hand and lead him to the window. I open the window and point to what is outside.

I have no teaching, but I carry on a conversation. (693)

This book serves as an accessible introduction to what Buber was pointing toward—not to a concept but to a living dialogue by listening faithfully and by responding authentically, heart/mind to heart/mind.

Visiting Buber

The following vignette, told by Phyllis A. Anderson (in a letter to the author), describes her meeting with Martin Buber in his home.

> In 1963 I had a grant to study in Israel for six weeks. I traveled there with a group directed by Professor Menahem Mansoor—at that time head of the Department of Hebrew and Semitic Studies, University of Wisconsin, Madison.
>
> Dr. Mansoor was well known in Israel and we were invited to have tea and a short meeting with Martin Buber at his home in Jerusalem. It was hot but the stone house had tiled floors, high ceilings, and window blinds that let the breeze through, but moderated the sunlight. Every room was lined, ceiling to floor with books and large library ladders on rollers, even the dining room. There was a very young child playing with a kitty. After tea we stood around the dining room and in came a frail, fragile looking old man in house shoes. The child crawled into his lap and he spoke briefly, then told us we could ask questions. We were all awed by the situation but there were questions. Finally, he indicated that he was tired, so only one more question. Someone asked, "Dr. Buber who do you think has been the greatest man in history?" Buber paused a moment, almost as if surprised and said quietly: "Why, there are *no* great men, only useful ones." Then he rose, smiled a gentle smile, bowed slightly, and shuffled out to the kitchen where women were preparing a meal. Our group exited in total silence.

The phrase "great men" can be used categorically in a way that reduces a person's uniqueness to a one-sided, formulaic catchword. Rather than "great" persons, Buber was more interested in meeting "useful" persons, persons who are capable of wholeheartedly responding to the unique particularities of the other. It is, therefore, somewhat counterproductive to try painting Buber heroically. Instead, we are most concerned with Buber's usefulness, the immediate applicability of his life's work to our ways of living and knowing. The life of dialogue is lived, not emulated. And, as we will see, it is grounded in the uniqueness of each person.

I and Thou (1923)

It is now more than seventy-five years since Buber first published the little book that was to become a monumental classic for philosophers, theologians, and comparative religionists. Only 120 pages long, *I and Thou (Ich und Du)* was written, as Buber said, in a type of "creative ecstasy" that was "impelled by an inward necessity." In the "Postscript" to *I and Thou* he continues: "This clarity was so manifestly suprapersonal in its nature that I at once knew I had to bear witness to it" (Smith, 123).

Among all of his works, this bearing witness remains Buber's masterpiece. Widely held as one of the most influential works in modern philosophy, *I and Thou* has attained the status of a little classic. Even in his later years Buber considered it the starting point of his dialogical philosophy. At once philosophic and poetic, it is the single text that generates his reputation in both professional and popular circles.

Because it challenges accepted modes of communication, and because of its dense language, Buber's little classic is also difficult to understand. The two available English translations are somewhat awkward, due in part to the lyrical-philosophical style of the original German. Reading *I and Thou* for the first time can be likened to walking into a foreign film halfway through without knowing the language of the subtitles. Little wonder, then, that the practice of Buber's genuine dialogue and responding responsibly are largely missing from today's public discourse.

The radical breakthrough in thought and lived experience represented by Buber's pioneering work, though, can be clarified.

In this book we approach the main body of *I and Thou* in six chapters, covering six of his central "principal addresses." Our last chapter covers Buber's "responses" to frequently asked questions, which he added several decades later, in his "Postscript." We take the liberty of recasting *I and Thou* (by means of abridgment, quotation, and paraphrase) to render its most meaningful insights into clear language. Of course, nothing can replace reading parts or the complete *I and Thou,* preferably in the original German.

Structure

Buber's classic is divided into a symphonic arrangement of three movements, each with subtly different internal meanings and rhythms. To accomplish our goal of unpacking Buber's language, this book too is arranged in three parts, paralleling the three parts of *I and Thou,* plus a "Postscript." In Part I Buber discusses what we will call his Generating (*I-Thou* and *I-It*) Grid in relation to "nature," "persons," and "spirit becoming forms." In Part II Buber traces two *interhuman realizations* of his Generating Grid: his vision of "true community" and the "real *I,*" which arise in relation to each other. In Part III Buber focuses attention on two *grounding prerequisites* of the Generating Grid: the "eternal *Thou*" and the personal act of "turning."

Part I, "The Generating Grid," focuses on the dynamic intersections of two primal word pairs and three relational realms that repeatedly intersect. To clarify Buber's initial address, Chapter 1 details his fundamental distinction between open, direct, mutual *I-Thou* relationships and knowing and using *I-It* relations. In Chapter 2 we discuss realms in which this polar reality arises: with nature, with humans, with spirit becoming forms, and, additionally, with the "eternal *Thou.*"

Part II, "Genuine Relationships," examines two reciprocal interhuman expressions of the *I and Thou* Grid: in community and through personal wholeness. It is in this section that the theme of turning first makes its appearance. Our focus in Chapter 3 is to describe and reflect upon the structures of genuine community; in

Chapter 4 we describe and discuss unified elements and manifestations of "the real *I*."

Part III, "Hallowing the Everyday," lays out two underlying interactions of living dialogue that continue being foundational to the *I and Thou* Grid. We focus here on Buber's discussion, in the third part of *I and Thou*, of the "eternal *Thou*," along with the practice of what Buber called turning. In this section it will become obvious that Buber's understanding of living dialogue is set in a transcendent context, on the one hand, and yet bears immediate and practical consequences, on the other hand.

Finally, we look at Buber's writing from almost forty years after publishing *I and Thou*, the 1958 "Postscript." In it he clarifies questions frequently asked over the years about *I and Thou*, adds new material, and becomes a bit more practice oriented. Following the structure of Buber's "Postscript," Chapter 7 distinguishes and discusses Buber's clarification of five repeated and interrelated questions arising from his *I and Thou* philosophy.

To present the material as clearly as possible, each of the seven chapters will follow a similar four-part pattern:

1. Buber's "principal address" is "spoken" through selected side-by-side translations of key passages from *I and Thou;*

2. Interpretive commentary is provided that clarifies Buber's teaching in a conversational manner;

3. An illustrative anecdote is selected from Buber's "Autobiographical Fragments" to explain further the significance of his "speaking"; and

4. Practice-oriented discussion questions are offered at the end of each chapter to facilitate personal applications and utilization of Buber's dialogical addresses.

How to Begin

Buber himself answers the question of how to begin reading *I and Thou*. In the "Postscript" he offers reader-oriented strategies that involve treating a text not as data, not as an object or an *It,* but as a *Thou.* To enter into a meaningful dialogue with a text, Buber proposes making the words immediately present, as if hearing the voice of the speaker; turning with one's whole being toward the speaker; adopting a "saying of *Thou*" attitude toward the text; and receiving the indivisible wholeness of something spoken. Buber would thus invite readers of *I and Thou* to read it dialogically and imaginatively.

But how does this way of reading work? Essentially a text becomes person-like, or a *"Thou,"* by virtue of its unique, personal address understood in a back-and-forth conversational movement. In summary form, reading a text from a Buberian perspective involves at least four dialogically oriented pointings. The first points to reading the text with open *receptivity,* to hearing a "living voice," which quickly moves readers to enter into active give-and-take dialogue with the author's voice. Then, the otherness of the text reflects back the reader's own historical and cultural *presuppositions.* The third pointing calls the reader to reflect on the *meaning* of the text. The reader then *applies* the text by sharing interpretations with a larger community of readers. In this way, through faithful openness and by returning again to the text with new questions, the reader is able to grow through ever-new dialogues with the unique person's words, thoughts, and feelings addressing him or her.

Through this lens a dialogic reader discovers and responds to links between personal life and textual insights. The activity of reading is pictured here taking place on a conversational field and involves reciprocal and reciprocating dialogues: between author and text, author and reader, and reader and text. A text, as visualized here, is not just a soliloquy or a monologue, nor is any one interpretation merely subjective. Rather, a fruitful reciprocity exists between *I and Thou,* Martin Buber, and the reader, with understanding located in their interplay. By entering into dialogue with *I and Thou,* as with each *Thou,* the reader's own voice becomes articulated more clearly.

Text as *Thou*

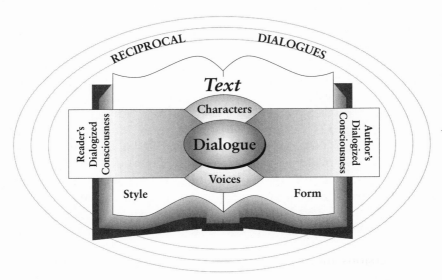

Two Translations

I and Thou was first published in German in 1923, and it was first translated into English by Ronald Gregor Smith in 1937. A second edition was then published in 1958, including several translation corrections and Buber's addition of the "Postscript." Then, in 1970, five years after Buber had died, *I and Thou* was retranslated into English by Walter Kaufmann at the request of Buber's son, Rafael.

Even a cursory comparison of these two translations reveals some rather important differences. Smith consistently translated the title word *Du* as *"Thou."* Kaufmann translates *Du* as "You," in a partial attempt to update and modernize Smith's translation. Although Kaufmann's title page retains the translation *I and Thou* (for *Ich und Du*), his Prologue opens with the title "I and You," a word he retains throughout the text. The multiple significances of this and other differences can hardly be overestimated and will be taken up again in the following chapters.

Introduction

I and Thou
Versions

SMITH (1937/1958)	ORIGINAL GERMAN (1923)	KAUFMANN (1970)
Thou	*Du*	You
All real living is meeting	*Alles wirkliche Leben ist Begegnung*	All actual life is encounter
Meeting	*Begegnung*	Encounter
Realize	*Verwirklichen*	Actualize
Turn	*Umkehr*	Return
Inclusion	*Umfassung*	Embracing

Because each translation has its strengths and weaknesses, when commenting on passages from *I and Thou* we juxtapose the two versions and, where important, compare each to the original German and, when necessary, suggest our own translation. Readers who become more familiar with the differences between the translations may wish to read just one or the other consistently but can still benefit in understanding and come closer to the layers of original meaning by reading and comparing Smith's and Kaufmann's versions.

We can imagine at this point a person asking, "What is the purpose of the side-by-side textual referencing? Wouldn't it be more appropriate if only the better translation, the one closest to Buber's intention, was quoted? And won't the side-by-side references slow a reader down?" Yes, but there is no single "better" translation. Each of them is flawed and each is correct in different respects. When quoting Buber, therefore, we include both, for the sake of completeness as well as for the sake of comparative clarity.

Although at times Smith's translation works better for key Buberian terms, it would be restrictive to favor one translation over the other. Rather than privileging Smith over Kaufmann, or vice versa, we will study Buber's classic through the eyes of both. This is especially significant for readers who do not know German, because comparing the translations at significant passages will further clarify Buber's intention.

Since *Martin Buber's I and Thou* is about *practicing* as well as *understanding* genuine dialogue—our "human birthright"—the lens used here is a dialogical one. As authors, having spent years reading, discussing, and teaching I and Thou at San José State University, we bring ourselves to the material as interactively as possible. Thus, whether used in classes, study groups, seminars, counseling situations, or religious settings, this book has the primary goal of offering breakthrough teachings for humanizing our lives. What all this finally comes to is simple and direct: The sought-for treasure, the fulfillment of existence, can be found right here in the midst of genuine dialogue.

PART I

THE GENERATING GRID

The world of *It* is set in the context of space
and time.

The world of *Thou* is not set in the context of
either of these.

The particular *Thou,* after the relational event
has run its course, is *bound* to become an *It.*

The particular *It,* by entering the relational
event, *may* become a *Thou.*

—MARTIN BUBER (Smith, 33)

Chapter 1

The Twofold World

There is no I taken in itself, but only the I of the primary
word *I-Thou* and the I of the primary word *I-It*.

"من" خالی ندارم . "من - این" یه واحد تعلیل ناپذیری،
و "من - تو"

One way to begin studying Buber's classic is to consider, for
a moment, a preliminary question: What do I need to know
before reading *I and Thou* that will assist me in my attempt to
understand it? Maurice Friedman, who has spent over fifty years
studying, interpreting, and translating the writings of Buber, was
once asked this question in a comparative religious studies seminar at San José State University. In response, Friedman said: "It
must be understood first that *Thou* is not an object but a *relationship*. If this is not understood, the rest of the book will not be
understood."

Rather than serving as an object of experience, *"Thou"*
points to the quality of genuine relationship in which partners are
mutually unique and whole. This living realization is neither subjective nor objective, but *interhuman*. It emerges from the place
that Buber calls the realm of "the between." This is why Buber
writes: "All real living is meeting." Genuine meeting occurs when
people enter dynamic solidarity with one another. This deep bonding is contained neither in one, nor the other, nor in the sum of
both—but becomes really present *between* them.

Primal Life Stands

What is common to every person, according to Buber, is lived speech, speech-with-meaning, speech through which we become *human* with other humans.[1] We enter the world dressed in speech. Buber's point of departure for what he later called "the life of dialogue" is the ever-renewing presence of alternative life stands. According to Buber, human life is lived in a continuous interplay between two primal "attitudes," or "ways of speaking"— *I-It* and *I-Thou*—with all that they involve. These life stands are certainly not, for Buber, absolute alternatives, but rather complementary opposites that continuously interchange with one another.

Each person lives in an *I-It—I-Thou* continuum, in continual alternations between the two basic life stands. In this light Buber suggests that what makes a person *human* is building, with others, a common world of "speech with meaning." If *I-It* indicates degrees of separation from others, *I-Thou* indicates a togetherness of close bonding. That is, we respond to whatever is encountered in ways that are either more objectifying and monological *(I-It)*, or more immediate, mutual, and dialogical *(I-Thou)*. Being *human* involves continually choosing one or the other modality of meeting and responding to whatever addresses and engages us.

In the beginning, therefore, it is crucial to grasp the fact that when Buber speaks of the two primal word pairs, he means to indicate two fundamental ways of responding to, or communicating with, whatever is before us. When we say "I," we use one or the other manner of speaking. Thus, according to Buber, by speaking either one or the other primal mode, we continually reposition ourselves relationally.

In *I-It* relations, for example, the other (whether a person, text, nature, or spirit) is objectified and reduced to the content of the observer's own experience. In *I-Thou* relationships, on the other hand, the other (friend, family, stranger) is invited to meet me where I stand, in open, mutual reciprocity. Both modes of speaking are necessary. While our lives in the world benefit in practical ways because of *I-It* relations, developing personal wholeness requires *I-Thou* relationships.

Indeed, according to Buber, one becomes *human* only in *I-Thou* relationships, for only these call a person into unique wholeness.

As Buber states, "I become through my relation to the *Thou;* as I become *I,* I say *Thou*" (Smith, 11). That is, I become genuinely *human* with and through *Thou.*

I-Thou and *I-It*

On the first page of *I and Thou* Buber introduces his now-famous distinction between *I-It* and *I-Thou,* which underlies the whole book. Buber's entire dialogical philosophy is grounded in these two word pairs, or two types of interactions. R. G. Smith translates the two "primary" words "*I-Thou*" (capitalized and italicized) and "*I-It*" (capitalized and italicized). For Kaufmann, on the other hand, the two "basic" word pairs are translated "I-You" and "I-It." Because Smith's translation is closer to Buber's intention, we will adopt his version of the word pairs throughout.[2]

SMITH, 3 *I-THOU* AND *I-IT*	KAUFMANN, 53 I-YOU AND I-IT
To man the world is twofold, in accordance with his twofold attitude.	The world is twofold for man in accordance with his twofold attitude.
The attitude of man is twofold, in accordance with the twofold nature of the primary words which he speaks.	The attitude of man is twofold in accordance with the two basic words he can speak.
The primary words are not isolated words, but combined words.	The basic words are not single words but word pairs.
The one primary word is the combination *I-Thou.*	One basic word is the word pair I-You.
The other primary word is the combination *I-It;* wherein, without a change in the primary word, one of the words *He* and *She* can replace *It.*	The other basic word is the word pair I-It: but this basic word is not changed when He or She takes the place of It.
Hence the *I* of man is also twofold.	Thus the I of man is also twofold.
For the *I* of the primary word *I-Thou* is a different I from that of the primary word *I-It.*	For the I of the basic word I-You is different from that in the basic word I-It.

In the opening verse-paragraph of *I and Thou,* Buber laid the cornerstone of his "life of dialogue." This passage has led some readers to question whether Buber affirms that there are really two distinct worlds (the world of *I-It* and the world of *I-Thou*). Buber addressed this question directly when he said that the world itself is not twofold. Instead, two ways of *standing* in the world, or *communicating* (translated above as a "twofold attitude") flow through each person into "the real world" of lived experience.[3]

These two word pairs are primal (primary, basic) because they establish two fundamental modes of speaking in the world.[4] There is no "I" taken by itself. "I" exists only in relation to the other, whether we turn to the other as wholly *Thou* or objectified *It.* Whoever speaks one of the primal words enters into the "I," the chosen subject position, and stands therein.[5] In *I-It* relations I remain outside these interactions by controlling the beginning, middle, and end, the subject discussed, and how it is defined. In *I-Thou* relationships, on the other hand, I yield control by fully entering into relationship naturally and spontaneously.

Two Primal Life Stands

I-IT RELATIONS	*I-THOU* RELATIONSHIPS
Never Spoken with the Whole Being	Spoken with the Whole Being
Experiencing/Using/Knowing	Event/Happening
In Space and Time	Spaceless/Timeless
One-sided: Singular	Two-sided: Mutual
Controlling	Yielding
Subject-Object Duality	Interhuman Betweenness

I-Thou Relationship

I-Thou interactions are direct and open moments of mutual presence between persons, according to Buber, and are necessary for becoming whole human beings. It is well to remember here that in *I-Thou* relationships, the *Thou* is not a pronoun that stands for a name. When "I" address you as *"Thou,"* I enter into direct relationship with you as a uniquely whole person, not merely as an identity.[6]

"I-Thou" thus refers to a two-sided event in which our personal uniqueness enters into relationship with another's personal uniqueness, as if a child has been laid in our arms and we are called upon to respond with our whole person. Certainly, Buber's ever-renewed reason for writing was his conviction that each of us is capable of entering into *I-Thou* relationships with one another, through which surprising and new dimensions of reality arise. Of course, there is no pure *I-Thou* relationship without an *I-It* point of reference. Nor can we have an *I-Thou* relationship with everyone, or in every situation. We can, however, remain open and willing to intend to enter *I-Thou* interactions with those of similar intentions.

But if a continuous *I-Thou* relationship is neither possible nor desirable, how frequently does it occur? In *Philosophical Interrogations* Buber addresses this question:

> Since the perfect I-Thou relation[ship] in general makes no statement concerning itself, I do not know how frequent or how rare it is.…For I believe that it can transform the human world, not into something perfect, but perhaps into something very much more human, according to the created meaning of [a person], than exists. (38–39)

It is important to recall that by *"Thou,"* Buber does not mean either "God" or "you" as an object of my perception, or "he," or "she," or "it," for that matter. Rather, with the word *"Du"* Buber refers to the presence of uniqueness and wholeness emerging from genuine listening and responsible responding. When I enter into real relationship with another as a *Thou*, I voluntarily become another's *Thou*. *I-Thou* relationship, then, is exclusive and momentary, cannot be held onto, and does not permanently hold. When Buber asked himself, What does one experience of the *Thou?* he gave two seemingly contradictory responses: "nothing" and "everything." By "nothing," he meant no particular object. By "everything," he meant the unique presence of wholeness.

Since Buber's philosophy is experiential and uniquely personal, a real-world example of engaging the *Thou* might best clarify his central concern. Asked to reflect on her experience of *I-Thou* mutuality, Jennifer Maione, a former student at San José State University, related a touchstone event unique in its particulars and yet parallel to many other human experiences.

> I recall a conversation that I believe was confirming for me as well as the person I was talking to. My freshman year in high school, a girl on my bus was let off near her house and as she crossed the street a car came over the hill and hit her. I didn't see it, but she was taken away in an ambulance and wasn't in school for a few days. We weren't very close, but we only lived right down the street from each other and had ridden the same bus to school for a couple of years. I don't remember what made me do it, but I got her phone number from another neighbor and gave her a call. I think I just genuinely wanted to make sure she was all right.
>
> We ended up talking for hours. What I remember most about our discussion is that she made me feel as though I had genuinely listened and offered her something no one else had. I think that I was the one person she really opened up to about her thoughts and fears regarding the accident. I couldn't tell you now all the things we said, but I know we talked for a long time and I know that I got off the phone feeling very good, unaware of how much time had passed, and wishing that the conversation didn't have to end.

In Buberian terms, each participant experiences mutual presence, a vital reciprocity, an elemental togetherness not restricted by time-awareness.

Directness and Wholeness

After discussing the central *I-Thou* axis of relationship, Buber delineates three behavioral characteristics of participants in genuine dialogue, that is, directness and wholeness, will and grace, and the presence of mutuality:

SMITH, 11
MEETING

KAUFMANN, 62
ENCOUNTER

The *Thou* meets me through grace—it is not found by seeking. But my speaking of the primary word to it is an act of my being, is indeed *the* act of my being.

The You encounters me by grace—it cannot be found by seeking. But that I speak the basic word to it is a deed of my whole being, is my essential deed.

The *Thou* meets me. But I step into direct relation with it. Hence the relation means being chosen and choosing, suffering and action in one; just as any action of the whole being, which means the suspension of all partial actions and consequently of all sensations of actions grounded only in their particular limitation, is bound to resemble suffering.

The You encounters me. But I enter into a direct relationship to it. Thus the relationship is election and electing, passive and active at once: An action of the whole being must approach passivity, for it does away with all partial actions and thus with any sense of action, which always depends on limited exertions.

The primary word *I-Thou* can be spoken only with the whole being. Concentration and fusion into the whole being can never take place through my agency, nor can it ever take place without me. I become through my relation to the *Thou;* as I become *I*, I say *Thou*.

The basic word I-You can be spoken only with one's whole being. The concentration and fusion into a whole being can never be accomplished by me, can never be accomplished without me. I require a You to become; becoming I, I say You.

All real living is meeting.

All actual life is encounter.

From this pivotal passage, delineating the undivided wholeness of genuine meeting (in the sense of engaging and being engaged), the rest of Buber's *I and Thou* proceeds. The decisive

21

single-sentence paragraph, "All real living is meeting" *(Begegnung)* is crucial for Buber, because genuine meeting requires an altogether different kind of attentiveness—a living relationship of whole person to whole person. "All real living is meeting" does not mean that the objective other is unreal, but that the *"It"* finds its reality when brought into the direct presence of an affirming *"I."*

Genuine meeting embodies directness and wholeness. By *directness* Buber means immediacy, presence without agendas. In his definition of *wholeness* Buber includes both "choosing" to enter relationship, and "being chosen" by one who also chooses to enter relationship. Dialogical wholeness, then, involves both "surrender and action." Smith translates the key German word *"Passion"* as "suffering"; Kaufmann translates *"Passion"* as "passive." But in this context *"Passion"* means more moving toward the behavior of "surrendering" into relationship.

Will and Grace

As Buber has indicated in various contexts, I become fully myself in and through relationship with the *Thou*: "I become through my relation[ship] to the *Thou*; as I become *I*, I say *Thou.*" To put it succinctly, when genuine meeting happens, my will and intentionality are passionately involved. Implications of this insight reverberate throughout the text.

Yet, no matter how much I "will" genuine relationship, finally the *Thou* meets me through the effective grace of reciprocal acts of compassion. Action and surrender, will and relational grace, generate the interactive immediacy of meeting. For Buber, *grace* is not a theological term but the spontaneously undetermined *presence of mutuality,* which cannot be activated by will alone. If "will and grace" provide the necessary preconditions for meeting, the "presence of mutuality" characterizes its genuine nature.

Presence of Mutuality

The I-Thou relationship, as well, is simultaneously "inclusive" and "exclusive." It is inclusive insofar as "the world dwells in me as an image" and "I dwell in it as a thing." But it is exclusive when, as Buber writes, the *Thou* steps forth and confronts me and "fills the heavens." When the relationship between "*I*" and "*Thou*" is genuine, there exists a mutual giving. "You say *Thou* to it and give yourself to it, it says *Thou* to you and gives itself to you" (Smith, 33). In other words, "*I*" and "*Thou*" give to one another in the mutual reciprocity between two persons. In this context, Buber writes:

SMITH, 15–16
MUTUAL

KAUFMANN, 67
RECIPROCITY

Relation is mutual. My *Thou* affects me, as I affect it. We are moulded by our pupils and built up by our works. The "bad" man, lightly touched by the holy primary word, becomes one who reveals. How we are educated by children and by animals! We live our lives inscrutably included within the streaming mutual life of the universe.

Relation is reciprocity. My You acts on me as I act on it. Our students teach us, our works form us. The "wicked" become a revelation when they are touched by the sacred basic word. How are we educated by children, by animals! Inscrutably involved, we live in the currents of universal reciprocity.

According to Buber, this primary togetherness—the mutual life of the universe—is formed by real immediacy. Therefore, genuine meeting involves mutual stand-taking and mutual self-giving. Needless to say, since genuine *I-Thou* relationships are mutually present, the reality of that relationship—meeting others and holding our ground in the meeting—cannot be reduced to a distinct or an abstract feeling, to an "emotion recollected in tranquility." But what should we understand here by "mutually present"?

Consider, for instance, Buber's understanding of love. Where does love occur? Inside a person or between persons? Buber writes that feelings may accompany love, but they do not constitute love. While feelings dwell *in* a person the way a person dwells *in* the world, a person in love dwells *in* the mutual presence of love. Real love is deep bonding between *I* and *Thou*, and a loving relationship proceeds from the voluntarily assumed "responsibility of an *I* for a *Thou*" (Smith, 14).

In this context it becomes clear that *I-Thou* moments consist not of two experiences dwelling distinctly in two persons but of a third dimension, the dimension of "the between," in which shared experience enlivens the *I-Thou* relationship:

"I"	THE BETWEEN	*"THOU"*
Uniquely Whole Person	Real Meeting Happens	Uniquely Whole Person
Becoming *I* Through *Thou*	Elemental Togetherness	Becoming *I* Through *Thou*
Turning Toward	Vital Reciprocity	Turning Toward
Unconditional Trust	Memorable Common Fruitfulness	Unconditional Trust
Existential Courage	Mutual Bonding	Existential Courage

The presence of mutuality, or "the between," is central to Buber's thought and to this text as well. While the interactive sphere of "the between" is vital to each chapter, it will receive more focused discussion in Chapters 3 and 4.

The "Eternal *Thou*"

One of Buber's most significant yet difficult insights in *I and Thou* he called the "eternal *Thou*." As he indicated on several occasions, the central tenet of his life's work was that the *I-Thou* relationship between persons intimately reflects the *I-Thou* relationship humans have with God. Genuine relationship with any *Thou* shows glimpses of the "eternal *Thou*."

Thus, Buber's use of the word *"Thou"* has a twofold referent: both a temporal *Thou* (who can become *It*) and the "eternal *Thou*" (who cannot become *It*). Early in Part I of *I and Thou*, we read a paragraph that Buber reiterates again in the middle of Part III:

SMITH, 6, 101 ETERNAL *THOU*	KAUFMANN, 57, 150 ETERNAL YOU
In every sphere in its own way, through each process of becoming that is present to us we look out toward the fringe of the eternal *Thou;* in each we are aware of a breath from the eternal *Thou;* in each *Thou* we address the eternal *Thou*.	In every sphere, through everything that becomes present to us, we gaze toward the train of the eternal You; in each we perceive a breath of it; in every You we address the eternal You, in every sphere according to its manner.

Kaufmann's decision to translate *"Du"* as "You" is especially inadequate when *"Du"* refers to the eternal *"Thou."* As we will discuss in Chapter 5, the "eternal *Thou*" is not to be regarded as a separate being who is brought into the relationship. In contrast to all other existing beings, the "eternal *Thou*" cannot be reduced to even the loftiest conceivable objective image. The eternal presence of God is instead glimpsed in the immediacy of relationship itself.

Reading through *I and Thou,* it thus becomes clear that Buber's dialogical stand is inseparable from his view that God not only can be glimpsed in genuine dialogue, but also reaches out to humans by penetrating the realm of the between. Here, we recall that the society to which Buber spoke was more homogeneous (and, arguably, hegemonic) than ours. The religious traditions that inform *I and Thou* are mainly Jewish and Christian, and the primary audience for the book practiced those faiths. Nevertheless, in a multicultural society Buber's dialogical life stand can still beneficially be practiced in either religious or humanistic contexts.

I-It Relations

Having addressed and elevated the primal *I-Thou* word pair, Buber acknowledges that "the exalted melancholy of our fate [is] that every *Thou* in our world must become an *It*" (Smith, 16). The intense presence of *Thou* moments inevitably flows away, becoming objects, frozen ideas relegated to past experience. The *I-It* relation refers to a necessarily one-sided experience of "knowing," "using," and putting things in "categories." In this objectified experience of the world, one does not venture outside self-reinforcing plans, schemes, and purposes.

While *I-Thou* relationships are wholly personal, *I-It* relations are intrinsically removed. *I-It* knowledge, or subject-object knowing, contains nothing other than socially conditioned categories of self-thought. Although the title *I and Thou* conveys the dialogical necessity of striving for genuine interaction with the world, Buber found it impossible to disregard the functional necessity of subject-object knowing. As he makes clear in *Philosophical Interrogations:*

> I have often indicated how much I prize science, so-called "objective knowledge." Without it there is no orientation in the world of "things" or of "phenomena," hence no orienting connection with the space-time sphere in which we have to pass our individualized life on earth. Without the splendid condensations, reductions, generalizations, symbolizations that science turns out, the handing down of a "given" order from generation to generation would be impossible. (48)

This "exalted melancholy," this ability to imagine that we are removed from the objects of our senses, leaves every *Thou* in the world fated to become a thing among things:

SMITH, 16–17 OBJECT AMONG OBJECTS	KAUFMANN, 68 OBJECT AMONG OBJECTS
It does not matter how exclusively present the *Thou* was in the direct relation. As soon as the relation has been worked out or has been permeated with a means, the *Thou* becomes an object among objects—perhaps the chief, but still one of them, fixed in its size and its limits.	However exclusively present it may have been in the direct relationship—as soon as the relationship has run its course or is permeated by *means,* the You becomes an object among objects, possibly the noblest one and yet one of them, assigned its measure and boundary.

There is a tinge of sadness beneath this recognition that the mind not only holds the capacity for ordering the world, but that it also elevates its own melancholy in this regard, even while it mechanically limits the capacity for the genuine unfolding of every human life.

Chrysalis and Butterfly

Buber describes the excruciating dynamics of this situation as analogous to the growing pains of a chrysalis and a butterfly:

SMITH, 17–18 CHRYSALIS AND BUTTERFLY	KAUFMANN, 69 CHRYSALIS AND BUTTERFLY
The *It* is the eternal chrysalis, the *Thou* the eternal butterfly—except that situations do not always follow one another in clear succession, but often there is a happening profoundly twofold, confusedly entangled.	The It is the chrysalis, the You the butterfly. Only it is not always as if these states took turns so neatly; often it is an intricately entangled series of events that is torturously dual.

The central relational event, the butterfly, inevitably becomes cocooned in the chrysalis of one-sided experiencing. *I-It* relations can be expressed in an almost infinite number of ways, and are all equally binding. A majority of human discourse is functionally of the *I-It* variety. That is, for the most part in my daily life I "use," "experience," "have," "do," "possess," "make," "compose," "figure out," and "inform" myself.

These types of expressions remain exclusively within one frame of reference and typically involve evaluation, judgment, justification, and association. While this form of discourse is necessary to serving the means and ends of individual commerce, *I-It* discourse alone is not enough to restore fuller humanness. Clinging to the chrysalis of objective experience, in fact, severely limits our ability to acknowledge what Buber considers our fundamental birthright.

The "Inborn *Thou*"

Toward the end of Part I, Buber reinforces his thesis that "all real living is meeting" by tracing the experience of an infant's emergence into relational consciousness. Using an expression that he would later reconsider, Buber writes, "In the beginning is relationship." That is, the prenatal life of a child is pure union with "the great mother—the individual, unshaped primordial world" (Smith, 29). It is from the natural combination of mother and child, Buber writes, that the primary awareness of *I-Thou* relationship begins.

In this perspective the presence of *Thou* corresponds to the development of the *human* being, and we are all born with an "inborn *Thou*"(Smith, 27). In the womb the child is enfolded in a natural relationship, the bonds of which are broken at birth. The "inborn *Thou*" of the child—our birthright, our fundamental heritage—is called forth from its original undifferentiated nature as his or her parents say *"Thou."* From the first moment of life, the child reaches out for contact, tactilely and visually confirming otherness. Only later, as the child learns, does the living relationship split into *I* and *It*.

The fact that a child initially recognizes the other as a *Thou* is based on the a priori concreteness of relationship. It is only through developing this "inborn *Thou*" that a child eventually becomes a person. In Buber's formulation the "inborn *Thou*" is both a "category of being" and a "model for the soul."

SMITH, 27
THE INBORN *THOU*

The inborn *Thou* is realized in the lived relations with that which meets it. The fact that this *Thou* can be known as what is over against the child, can be taken up in exclusiveness, and finally can be addressed with the primary word, is based on the *a priori* of relation.

KAUFMANN, 78–79
THE INNATE YOU

In the relationships through which we live, the innate You is realized in the You we encounter: that this, comprehended as a being we confront and accepted as exclusive, can finally be addressed with the basic word, has its ground in the *a priori* of relation.

Buber speaks subtly here. It is because the lived experience of the *Thou* is both a priori and inborn that Buber placed it "in the beginning." Buber does not speak here in a theological sense but rather in the phylogenetic sense. That is, just as the relationship between a person and the moon precedes the idea of the moon existing by itself, so the *I-Thou* relationship comes before the self-existence of either an *I* or a *Thou* alone.[7]

Through seeing, hearing, and touching, writes Buber, a child finds his or her own world. The "inborn *Thou*" expresses itself as the child reaches out for contact. According to Buber, the "inborn *Thou*" manifests only through entering into relationship with another *Thou*. As the child becomes conscious of "I," by learning to perceive his or her separateness from what is reached for (whether a teddy bear or a tea pot), the child learns to form objectifying relationships. From this separation the child confronts the world.

For Buber, then:

- The *I-Thou* relationship comes first, and the *I-It* relation emerges from it;

- The *I-It* is the "eternal chrysalis"; the *I-Thou* is the "eternal butterfly";

- The *I-Thou* continually becomes *I-It;* and only at times is the *It* capable of returning to the *Thou;*

- The *I-It* need not become the *I-Thou;* yet, to truly become a human person, one must meet the world as *Thou;* and

- The "inborn *Thou*" continues throughout life to seek genuine meeting.

The Subject-Object World

Buber concludes Part I of *I and Thou* by gathering his initial themes together and briefly rehearsing them. The *Thou* comes to you and addresses you in order to bring you forward into the world. Necessarily, the world of *It* is a world of things, processes, characteristics, and objects that are continuously divisible. An individual who primarily speaks *I-It* observes things as objects, arranges them, orders them, separates them, and connects them without necessarily feeling the weight of their importance. By classifying and formulating properties into concepts, we order objects into causal systems. Describing this world of *It,* which is set in the context of space and time, Buber writes:

SMITH, 33–34 THE WORLD OF *IT*	KAUFMANN 84–85 THE IT-WORLD
The world of *It* [is] the world in which he has to live, and in which it is comfortable to live, as the world, indeed, which offers him all manner of incitements and excitements, activity and knowledge. In this chronicle of solid benefits the moments of the *Thou* appear as strange lyric and dramatic episodes.	The It-world [is] the world in which one has to live and also can live comfortably—and that even offers us all sorts of stimulations and excitements, activities and knowledge. In this firm and wholesome chronicle the You-moments appear as queer lyric-dramatic episodes.

In the world of *It,* an individual perceives beings and actions as things and occurrences composed of properties and moments, as posited in spatial and temporal networks, compared and measured against other things. In the *It*-world, one experiences an object through the filter of one's perception: "It allows itself to be accepted by you, but does not give itself to you" (Smith, 35). In other words, there is an ever-recurring distance between one's self and the world of things.

Having said this, it is important to remember that, inevitably, interactions occur between the *It*-world and the *Thou*-world. In everyday life the two are often intertwined. Of necessity, a *Thou* becomes an *It* and an *It* may become a *Thou.* This switching can be almost instant or gradual, and it reflects a transformation of one's life orientation from being fully present to reflecting on a past moment, or from being concerned with this object against that object to entering into relationship.

As the *Thou* fades from relationship, *Thou* becomes an *It*-for-itself until becoming an *It* to an "I" as an object of experience. The subjective "I" cannot remain independent but becomes a subject by virtue of an *It* to define itself against. In other words, the "I" is defined by its relational, or lack thereof, orientation to the world.

Summarizing the ambiguity of the human situation, Buber concludes Part I by indicating that every particular *Thou* is bound to become *It:* "Without *It* a [a person] cannot live. But [one] who lives with *It* alone is not a [person]" (Smith, 34). While a person cannot become fully human without a *Thou,* a human being cannot live without *It.* Buber himself lived much of his life in the *It*-world of gathering materials and analyzing their meanings across disciplines.

Meeting Buber

Maurice Friedman, who knew Martin Buber and who translated and interpreted many of Buber's writings, has written a definitive three-volume biography entitled *Martin Buber's Life and Work,* along with a one-volume biography entitled *Encounter on the Narrow Ridge.* He has also written the best scholarly introduction to Buber's work: *Martin Buber: The Life of Dialogue.*

For years, Friedman reports, people have asked him what kind of person Martin Buber was. It is as if, Friedman remarks, people really want to know if Buber completely lived the dialogical life. Friedman often responds to this type of question by repeating what Buber said of Albert Schweitzer: "He's no saint, but I know him as a true man."

"My trust in Buber," Friedman writes, "began six years prior to meeting him when I first read *I and Thou.*" While Friedman worked on his doctoral dissertation on Buber's thought at the University of Chicago, Buber wrote to offer his help with the manuscript. Buber asked Friedman to write an account of his life without withholding and without analysis, suggesting that he would then know how to help the manuscript along. It was at that point, Friedman writes, that their relationship entered the human fullness of trust.

When Friedman first met Buber in person, on October 31, 1950, at the Jewish Theological Seminary in New York, Buber welcomed him by looking deeply into his eyes while taking his hand. Friedman's initial response was to feel how totally "other" Buber seemed. His eyes were of a depth, gentleness, and directness that Friedman had never before, or since, encountered. Upon reflection, Friedman realized that when he looked into Buber's eyes, he experienced that Buber really included him and thereby placed a demand on him to be fully present.

As they talked, Buber told Friedman of his meeting several days before with T. S. Eliot in London. They had been brought together by R. G. Smith. When Friedman asked Buber whether he did not find his own opinions different from those of Eliot, Buber replied: "When I meet a man I am not concerned with opinions but with the man." Friedman took this response as a reproach and a corrective pointer to what is really important. In *The Life of Dialogue*, which Buber called "a remarkable achievement," using Buber's language Friedman summarizes what Buber means by "the unbroken perseverance in dialogue":

The Life of Dialogue

A "LIVING UNITY"

"This life is part of our birthright as human beings for only through it can we obtain authentic human existence."

- The Sphere of the Between
- Mutual Confirmation
- Making the Other Present
- Overcoming Appearances
- Experiencing the Other's Side
- A Direction of Movement
- Toward Personal Wholeness
- Responsible Decision-making
- Realistic Trust

"But this birthright cannot be simply inherited, it must be earned" (97).

Genuine Dialogue

Inevitably, discussions of Part I of *I and Thou* lead to Buber's central concern for the liberating presence of "genuine dialogue." When two people completely meet one another, by grace authentic dialogue occurs beyond the reifying reach of either. Buber expanded this discussion in a subsequent work. In response to what he called a crisis of trust (provoked by monological decisions), and giving a further context to what he began describing in *I and Thou,* in an essay "Dialogue" (first published in 1929 and included in *Between Man and Man,* 19) he distinguishes three realms of dialogue: genuine, technical, and monological.

1. **Genuine Dialogue:** "Whether spoken or silent...each of the participants really has in mind the other or others in their present and particular being and turns to them with the intention of establishing a living mutual relation[ship] between himself and them."

2. **Technical Dialogue:** That communication which is "prompted solely by the need of objective understanding."

3. **Monologue Disguised as Dialogue:** That situation in which "two or more men, meeting in space, speak each with himself in strangely tortuous and circuitous ways and yet imagine they have escaped the torment of being thrown back on their own resources."

Dialogue becomes *genuine* when each of the participants is fully present to the other or others, openly attentive to all voices, and willing to be nonjudgmental. Dialogue becomes *technical* when the need to understand something, or gain information, is the focal point of the exchange. Dialogue becomes in fact *monologue* when one participant is only interested in imposing his or her point of view to the exclusion of all other views. Lacking real otherness, monologue eliminates the possibility of being surprised. Practically speaking, these distinctions significantly affect human behavior. Genuine dialogue moves beyond the exchange of informational content, beyond simultaneous or dueling monologues, to an immediate, direct engaging and being engaged in which attentive listening and inclusive responding flow back and forth.

Consequently, genuine dialogue is not possible without mutual engagement. Buber recognized that "mutuality" occurs in "real" conversations in brief moments where people, as it were, "happen" to and for each other. In *Between Man and Man,* Buber provides a concrete example of this phenomenon:

> In the deadly crush of an air-raid shelter the glance of two strangers suddenly meet for a second in astonishing and unrelated mutuality; when the All Clear sounds it is forgotten; and yet it did happen, in a realm which existed only for that moment. (204)

Although fleeting, these dialogic moments (which "disappear in the moment of their appearance") bear with them life's deepest significations.

Meetings

To help take us inside Buber's dialogical process, in each chapter we include an autobiographical fragment (moments that exercised a decisive influence on his thinking) from Buber's collection of personal anecdotes entitled *Meetings*. In *Encounter on the Narrow Ridge* Friedman describes Buber's autobiographical anecdotes with an enticing image:

> Some of the most profound of Buber's hard-won insights are contained within them like a vein of gold in marble. They await extraction by those who wrestle and contend with them until they are compelled to divulge their secret. (379)

The following sketch, quoted from Buber's *Meetings*, is intended to take us inside Buber's dialogical process by fomenting, as Friedman suggests they might in his introduction to Buber's anecdotes, group discussions and interactions.

Vienna

I spent my first year of university studies in Vienna, the city of my birth and my earliest childhood. The detached, flat memory images appear out of the great corporal context like slides of a magic lantern, but also many districts that I could not have seen address me as acquaintances. This original home of mine, now foreign, taught me daily, although still in unclear language, that I had to accept the world and let myself be accepted by it; it was indeed ready to be accepted. Something was established at that time that in later years could not become recast through any of the problematics of the age.

The lectures of those two semesters, even the significant scholarly ones, did not have a decisive effect on me. Only some seminars into which I had prematurely flung myself, rather the seminary as such, immediately exerted a strong influence: the regulated and yet free intercourse between teacher and students, the common interpretations of texts, in which the master at times took part with a rare humility, as if he too were learning something new, and the liberated exchange of question and answer in the midst of all scholastic fluency—all this disclosed to me, more intimately than anything that I read in a book, the true actuality of the spirit, as a "between."

What affected me most strongly, however, was the Burgtheater into which at times, day after day, I rushed up three flights after several hours of "posting myself" in order to capture a place in the highest gallery. When far below in front of me the curtain went up and I might then look at the events of the dramatic agon as, even if in play, taking here and now, it was the word, the "rightly" spoken human word that I received into myself, in the most real sense. Speech here first, in this world of fiction as fiction, won its adequacy; certainly it appeared heightened, but heightened to itself. It was only a matter of time, however, until—as always happened—someone fell for a while into recitation, a "noble" recitation. Then, along with the genuine spokenness of speech, dialogical speech or even monological (in so far as the monologue was just an addressing of one's own person as a fellow man and no recitation), this whole world, mysteriously built out of the surprise and law, was shattered for me—until after some moments it arose anew with the return of the over-against.

Since then it has sometimes come to pass, in the midst of the casualness of the everyday, that while I was sitting in the garden of an inn in the countryside of Vienna, a conversation penetrated to me from a neighboring table (perhaps an argument over falling prices by two market wives taking a rest), in which I perceived the spokenness of speech, sound becoming "Each-Other." (30–32)

Rethink these life events for a moment. Notice a variety of different teachers. First, Buber's original home, in unclear language, taught him to accept the world and to let himself be accepted by it. Second, the university seminars opened for him the "free intercourse between teacher and students" as they interpreted texts together. But what affected Buber most was the theater with its "rightly spoken human word." Dialogic speech appeared heightened. The genuine spokenness of dialogic speech entered him and, after departing, "arose anew with the return of the over-against." Through the spokenness of speech, Buber discovered the other; discovering the other, Buber recognized himself.

Practice Exercises

The first chapter of *I and Thou* raises many questions that continue to elude and challenge readers interested in Buber's work. Is the *I-It* relation ever more than just an experience? Does an *I-Thou* relationship become an *I-It* relation as soon as we give the other a gender classification, reducing the *Thou* to a "he" or a "she"? Is there something essentially necessary about seeing the physical presence of the other for a genuine dialogue to take place? Or is it possible to have a genuine dialogue over the phone or in e-mail?

We recommend two practices for responding to these questions. First, in dialogue circles, community and peer groups interested in discussing the implications of Buber's philosophy meet one another and exchange viewpoints. Dialogue circles (of six to twelve persons) in and outside of class settings promote personal conversations about putting dialogue into practice and are themselves practice dialogues.

Second, in dialogue journals we can record thoughts, questions, insights, and significant interactions that help us to develop (1) our own subjectivities, and (2) our inter-subjective exchanges with others. Professor Friedman has written that for years he asked students to keep a personal academic journal as a self-examination and a class examination.

The journal has four steps: (1) selecting a reading and writing it down; (2) rephrasing the reading to make personal sense of it; (3) responding—both intellectually and emotionally—to ideas it contains; and (4) relating the reflections to personal circumstances. A dialogue journal may be far less ambitious than this. For now, a suggested practice question can begin the journal process. The questions, of course, can lead anywhere, without monological restraint.

Suggested Questions

1. If I choose to live dialogue, how (with what attitude) do I say *Thou*?

2. In small groups introduce yourselves to one another. Listen to your listening and notice stereotypes that arise in your mind; try to listen past them. Talk about a situation in which you've lost your sense of time in dialogue. Write what you remember and what you found most significant about it. After small-group discussions, return to the full group to share insights.

3. Small groups might wish to consider these personal questions: What life stand are you taking when you evaluate, judge, or categorize individuals? What determines this life stand?

4. Describe in your own words Buber's distinction between the two primal life stands: *I-Thou* and *I-It*. Use examples from your life to illustrate the distinction.

5. Select a person in the group to read and discuss Buber's story "Vienna." The group may wish to discuss questions such as the following:

   - What did your home life teach you of significance?

   - In what ways has your relationship to real teachers helped shape you?

   - What was the significance for the young Buber of hearing the "genuine spokenness of speech"?

   - In what ways can you imagine the "spokenness of speech" becoming "Each-Other"?

6. When and how do you think you *really* learn something about another person?

Notes

1. At the time that *I and Thou* was first translated (1937), the word *man* was used to indicate *all* human beings. Buber's use of "man" is evident throughout his text. It is necessary, therefore, to remember that the German word translated as "man," *Mensch,* refers not to maleness but rather to human being. *Mensch,* thus, refers to both men and women in their humanness.

2. *Du* is difficult to translate. While Smith translates *Du* as *"Thou,"* Kaufmann translates *Du* as "You." Kaufmann argues that *"Thou"* has become uncommon in the English language and suggests that it has taken on religious implications. Kaufmann's use of the pronoun *You* attempted to prevent readers from assuming that Buber's *"Thou"* meant God. At the same time, Kaufmann's "You" loses some of the intimate closeness suggested by Buber's *"Du."* It is important to remember, for instance, that the word *Du* was rarely spoken in Buber's time. It was used to address people toward whom one felt very close, to describe a relationship that had a past, a present, and potential for a future. Before one would go through the process of formally introducing the *Du* into a

relationship, one had to be sure that the other person felt the same about the relation. Further, a relationship in which the *Du* was spoken had a sense of commitment. That is, each would be there for the other person no matter what might happen. *You* in the English language does not bear the same meanings.

Since the English language does not have the distinction contained in the German language between *Du* (referring to close relationships) and *Sie* (referring to formal friends or strangers), Kaufmann uses "You." The distinction here is crucial. Furthermore, in the German language the person addressed is referred to as either *Du* or *Sie* (each capitalized), while the I *(ich)* is always in the lower case. This is exactly opposite to the way one writes and conceptualizes in English, where "I" is always in the upper case, while "you" is always in the lower case.

3. Since Buber anchors everything that he will say in *I and Thou* in this opening passage, let us consider more closely what he meant by "twofold attitude" *(Haltung). Haltung* refers to a person's stance in the world. It is reflected by the difference between two primary, or grounding, words *(grundworte)* that one speaks: *I-Thou* and *I-It.* But the translation "attitude," used by Smith and Kaufmann, is too psychologically oriented. The German word *Haltung* is more relational. It refers to the way I associate myself to what is present with me, that is, to my basic bearing, or life orientation.

4. Buber's foundational distinction is clearer in German between *I-Thou* relationship *(Ich-Du Beziehung)* and *I-It* relation *(Ich-Es Verhältnis).* The difference between *Beziehung and Verhältnis* is crucial for understanding *I and Thou*'s emphasis on living two-sided events rather than one-sided experiences. Unfortunately, both words are translated by Smith, and at times by Kaufmann, as "relation." However, *Beziehung* means "relationship" between persons that includes past, present, and future dimensions.

On the other hand, *Verhältnis* refers to a "relation" of physical proximity only. For example, two billiard balls can be said to be in relation to each other on a pool table. Yet, they have no interpersonal relationship with each other. In Buber's view there is constant, conductive motion (in both directions) between *I-Thou* relationships and *I-It* relations. It is the melancholy of human fate that every *Thou* becomes an *It.* Yet, finally, movement from *I-It* to *I-Thou* is fundamental to human wholeness, not to mention fundamental for hallowing the everyday.

5. These two life stands are primal, or basic, because they constitute what is most fundamental about human life. The one primal word

pair, the combination *I-Thou (Ich-Du)*, is spoken with one's whole being. The other primal word pair, the combination *I-It (Ich-Es)*, is never spoken with one's whole being. Hence, my "I" is affected differently by *Thou* than by *It*. The "I" of *I-Thou* relationship is fully present, whereas the "I" of *I-It* individuality is never fully present.

During the time when Smith was first translating *Ich und Du*, Buber wrote to him that the *"Thou,"* while it cannot be spoken about, establishes relationship. Therefore, to remain as close to Buber's intention as possible, we will consistently follow Smith's translation of the two word pairs as *I-Thou* and *I-It*.

6. In *The Philosophy of Martin Buber*, Buber writes that "the concept of relationship *(Beziehung)*...opens the possibility—only the possibility, but this really—of the latency [of relationship]. Two friends, two lovers must, to be sure, experience ever again how the I-Thou is succeeded by an I-He or I-She" (705). In a later book, *The Knowledge of Man* (1965), Buber found it necessary to undergird his *I-Thou* and *I-It* distinction with a further insight. There, Buber went on to say that two primary movements, "distance" and "relationship," distinguish the human species from animals, and ground the division of *I-Thou* and *I-It*.

The first movement is the primal setting at a distance, by which Buber did not mean mere physical distance. Rather, he was referring to the *uniqueness* and *wholeness* of what comes into our presence. By thickening the distance between self and the other, I come to recognize you as a particular person. While distancing is a precondition for entering into relationship, the second movement does not always follow. Indeed, genuine relationship *(Beziehung)* involves a dynamic turning toward the one who is present with us.

Although Buber differentiates between *I-Thou* relationships and *I-It* relations as the two primal life stands, or ways of communicating in the world, it is important to remember the necessity of their interrelationship. Buber is not a dualist—he does not say *I-Thou* "versus" *I-It*. Rather, he speaks of *I-Thou* "and" *I-It* as modes of living that continually flow into and emerge from one another. We are never entirely located in the one or the other. From Buber's perspective, distancing and relating are not once and for all, but continuously alternate.

7. In a series of lectures given between January 15 and March 12, 1922, "Religion as Presence" (included in Rivka Horwitz's *Buber's Way to "I and Thou"*), Buber presented many of the themes that appear in *I*

and Thou. For instance, in a section of Lecture Five titled "Development of the Child," he writes:

> The primary act of the child, who reaches over the undifferentiated creation and so to speak out of and away from it, is the reaching for a Thou—and not only for a certain Thou that is experienced, such as the mother or an object, but for the Thou, for the still nameless, still unknown, undetermined Thou pure and simple. (80)

What Buber understands by the "inborn *Thou*" is precisely expressed here as "the still nameless, still unknown, undetermined Thou."

Chapter 2

Three Relational Realms

The spheres in which the world of relation is built are three. First, our life with nature....Second, our life with men....Third, our life with spiritual beings.

Chapter 1 introduced Buber's first principal address: "To man the relation to the world is twofold." Following this primary premise, it became apparent that for Buber

- The world itself is not twofold, but our perception of it is twofold;

- *I-Thou* relationships are direct, open, mutual, and present;

- *I-It* is a one-sided experience of knowing, using, and categorizing people and things;

- Both ways of relating are necessary for human life;

- A person ideally lives in a healthy alternation between the one and the other primary words;

- The *I-Thou* comes first; and the *I-It* grows out of it; and

- *I-Thou* again and again becomes *I-It*.

It is helpful to realize that a reciprocal dynamic exists between Chapter 1's two primal life stands and Buber's three relational realms, described in Chapter 2. Buber's Generating Grid embodies and describes the dynamics between the relational realms and the primal word pairs. This Generating Grid's relational interactions between humans and nature, humans and other people, and humans and spirit underlie the rest of the book.

All Real Living Is Meeting

All three of these relational realms open the possibility of genuine dialogue, as Buber makes clear in two mutually supporting phrases: "I become through my relation to the *Thou*" and "All real living is meeting" (Smith, 11). Smith's translation here more accurately captures Buber's intention than Kaufmann's does, especially when placed in the context of Buber's other writings, where again and again the point is made that I become wholly, uniquely, personally myself through engaging others. Through real meetings with a *Thou,* I become an *I!* As we will see, Buber's formulation is not limited to the realm of interhuman relationships.

By "meeting" *(Begegnung),* Buber means the event that actually takes place when one steps into a mutual "relationship" *(Beziehung)* and reciprocally meets *"Thou"* in the present moment, whole person to whole person. Indeed, the living actuality of meeting always takes place in the present moment. That is, meeting *Thou happens,* and only after *Thou* becomes *It* do we speak of meeting in other verb tenses, as "having happened" or "had happened."

When the event of meeting is past, when the *I-Thou* butterfly has been chrysalised into I-She, or I-He, or other forms of *I-It,* the possibility of relationship still continues, and genuine relationship deepens through everyday interactions between moments of *I-Thou* meetings. To an observer open to genuine dialogue, the day-to-day *I-It* experiences continually show glimpses of potentially deep encounters.

Genuine meeting, for Buber, is immediate, personal, and reciprocal. The *Thou* of this meeting is not restricted to a person but includes animals, aesthetic objects, nature, inspirited forms, and God. Through entering into a genuine dialogic relationship with the *Thou* in any form, I am no longer subject to causality and fate, no longer determined by space and time. Indeed, genuine meeting does not take place primarily in space and time; rather, space and time take place within genuine meeting. When the events referred to as grace and will combine to place my identity on the *I-Thou* axis of being, my sense of selfhood no longer depends primarily on the objectified realm of daily *I-It* interactions.

The Central Relational Event

When Buber said that he takes a person by the hand and leads him or her to the window, opens the window, and points to what is outside, we can imagine asking the question: To what was Buber pointing? Buber's response to this question can be gleaned

Figure 2–1. The Central Relational Event

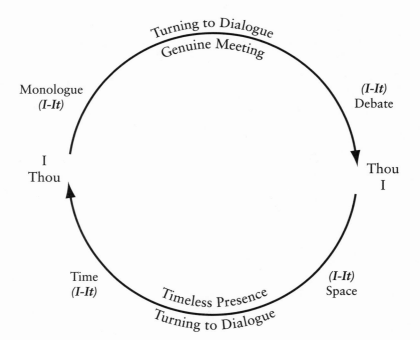

from his comment that, despite certain normative limitations, people can enter into "genuine dialogue with one another."

Genuine meeting happens in timeless presence when *"I"* and *"Thou"* each become reciprocally present. Decisive for Buber, the central relational event of *I-Thou* dialogue cannot be taught or transmitted. In Part III of *I and Thou* Buber writes that the simple fact of going forth into relationship "can only be indicated—by drawing a circle that excludes everything else. Then the one thing needful becomes visible: the total acceptance of the present" (Kaufmann, 126).

Mismeeting

To better understand what Buber means by *meeting,* and why it was so important to him, consider what occurs when meeting fails to happen. "Mismeeting," for Buber, occurs when seeming to be genuine or imposing one's will on another takes precedence over being spontaneously none other than oneself. Like the totality of Buber's world view, the concept of mismeeting was drawn from his own experience.

Martin Buber was born in Vienna in 1878; he lived with his parents in a house under which flowed the Danube Canal. He used to stand looking at the canal with a sense that nothing could disturb the serene way of life that he enjoyed. Then, suddenly, his mother disappeared. For years no one, including his father, knew where she had gone. Much later it was discovered that she had eloped with an army officer, left for Russia, and raised a new family there.

Soon after his mother's disappearance, the three-year-old Buber was sent to live with his paternal grandparents, Solomon and Adele Buber, who owned a large estate near Lvov, Austria. They were people of high rank, well educated, and leaders in the community. Solomon and Adele Buber became both parents and teachers for the young Martin.

Even though no one was sure where Buber's mother had gone, Buber's grandparents tried to keep his hopes alive. Before the age of four, though, while playing on a balcony, a neighboring girl told him what the adults in his life would not. In *Meetings,* Buber writes:

> We both leaned on the railing. I cannot remember that I spoke of my mother to my older comrade. But I hear still how the big girl said to me: "No, she will never come back." I know that I remained silent, but also that I cherished no doubt of the truth of the spoken words. It remained fixed in me; from year to year it cleaved ever more to my heart, but after more than ten years I had begun to perceive it as something that concerned not only me, but all men. (18)

Thirty years later, when Buber did meet his mother again, their encounter was racked with anxiety. Their distance, her abandonment of him, and her alternative life reinforced the gulf between them.

Later, Buber coined the word *Vergegnung*—"mismeeting"— to designate the failure of real interactive mutuality between persons. As he indicated himself, much of what he learned about genuine meeting over the course of his life had its origin in that hour on the balcony. His sense of genuine meeting, in other words, arose from his painful awareness of the ubiquity of mismeeting, of its universal affect on all humans. One thing that Buber's childhood experience of mismeeting taught him—which he only realized later—was that a sense of insecurity is often associated with meeting the *Thou.* Genuine meeting, Buber discovered, requires unconditional trust, a willingness to be vulnerable to the other.

Just as we live in a continuous cycle between awareness of *I-Thou* relationships and *I-It* relations, we live in a continuous exchange between meeting and mismeeting. When, instead of responding to others as unique persons, we treat them as objects among objects, as projected images that fit the structure of our knowledge, we disrupt our own capacity to encounter the *Thou* of others.

In both the history of cultures and the life span of individuals, a healthy alternation between *I-Thou* meetings and *I-It* mismeetings is interrupted when humans and institutions overemphasize or valorize the *I-It* approach to experience. To affect the renewal of genuine dialogue, interhuman trust is needed. Trusting a person means, at least for Buber, that whatever this person may do, say, or become, I am willing to accept him or her not as an object of my experience but as a human being.

MISMEETING *(Vergegnung)*	MEETING *(Begegnung)*
Dismissing the Other	Accepting the Other
• Labeling	• As a unique person
• Misrepresenting	• As a co-equal person
Misrecognizing the Other	Affirming the Other
• Culturally induced stereotypes	• Addressing and responding
• Judging the other	even through tensions
Miscommunicating with the Other	Confirming the Other
• Distorting	• Accepting and affirming,
• Misunderstanding	even while withstanding

The Supreme Meeting

In contrast to mismeeting, the most powerful moments of dialogue, when "deep calls unto deep," occur on a narrow ridge between subject and object, where *I* and *Thou* meet. Often, when reading and pondering portions of *I and Thou,* a few lines will light up and signal a unity that embraces Buber's central teaching throughout. Consider the following passage from Part III:

SMITH, 109
THE SUPREME MEETING

What is the eternal, primal phenomenon, present here and now, of that which we term revelation? It is the phenomenon that a man does not pass, from the moment of the supreme meeting, as the same being as he entered into it. The moment of meeting is not an "experience" that stirs in the receptive soul and grows to perfect blessedness; rather, in that moment something happens to the man. At times it is like a light breath, at times like a wrestling-bout, but always—it *happens.* The man who emerges from the act of pure relation that so involves his being has now in his being something more that has grown in him, of which he did not know before and whose origin he is not rightly able to indicate.

KAUFMANN, 157–58
THE SUPREME ENCOUNTER

What is that is eternal: the primal phenomenon, present in the here and now, of what we call revelation? It is man's emerging from the moment of the supreme encounter, entering into it. The moment of encounter is not a "living experience" that stirs in the receptive soul and blissfully rounds itself out: something happens to man. At times it is like feeling a breath and at times like a wrestling match; no matter: something happens. The man who steps out of the essential act of pure relation has something more in his being, something new has grown there of which he did not know before and for whose origin he lacks any suitable words.

Genuine relationship between persons is an unanticipated occurrence, a spontaneously reciprocal event. Rather than a self-contained "experience," the moment of meeting activates, between persons, the emergence of something new, beyond words.[1] In almost graphic language, Buber offers an interpretation of the "essential act of pure relation[ship] in three dimensions": the fullness of real mutuality, the inexpressible confirmation of meaning, and the fact that meaning is received in real life.

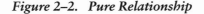

Figure 2–2. Pure Relationship

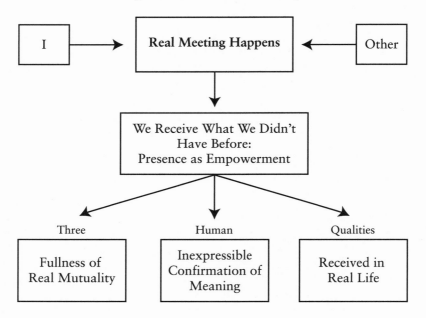

In other words, genuine meeting does not "switch off" in the chrysalis stage of relationship. Rather, it infuses a person's life because the effect of real meeting is immediate and profoundly personal. Unlike most "experiences" that "stir in a person's soul" and eventually grow "into blessedness," *I-Thou* encounters cannot be traced to an origin or a cause. If they could, the act of tracing them would immediately throw them into the realm of *I-It* again.

It follows from what has been said that entering into immediate relationship with a *Thou* represents a high peak of relational life, a sudden flash that illumines a person's way. In other words, when two (or more) persons simultaneously step into direct relationship, a new quality of communication springs forth. But if it cannot be traced to a cause, where does that communication of real relationship and genuine meeting occur?

Nature/Persons/Spirit

While Buber's first principle distinguishes two primal ways of communicating with the world, his second principle depicts three non-hierarchal relational realms in which meetings occur: (1) in our unspoken life with nature; (2) in our life with humans, through speech; and (3) in our life with "spirit becoming forms" (translated by Smith and Kaufmann as "spiritual beings"), beyond speech.

SMITH, 6
THREE SPHERES

The spheres in which the world of relation arises are three.

First, our life with nature. There the relation sways in gloom, beneath the level of speech. Creatures live and move over against us, but cannot come to us, and when we address them as *Thou,* our words cling to the threshold of speech.

Second, our life with men. There the relation is open and in the form of speech. We can give and accept the *Thou.*

Third, our life with spiritual beings. There the relation is clouded, yet it discloses itself; it does not use speech, yet begets it. We perceive no *Thou,* but none the less we feel we are addressed and we answer—forming, thinking, acting. We speak the primary word with our being, though we cannot utter *Thou* with our lips.

KAUFMANN, 56–57
THREE SPHERES

Three are the spheres in which the world of relation arises.

The first: life with nature. Here the relation vibrates in the dark and remains below language. The creatures stir across from us, but they are unable to come to us, and the You we say to them sticks to the threshold of language.

The second: life with men. Here the relation is manifest and enters language. We can give and receive the You.

The third: life with spiritual beings. Here the relation is wrapped in a cloud but reveals itself, it lacks but creates language. We hear no You and yet feel addressed; we answer—creating, thinking, acting: with our being we speak the basic word, unable to say You with our mouth.

In and through each of these three realms it is possible to enter a genuine *I-Thou* relationship, but the form and movement of that relationship in each of the realms is somewhat different. Usually, we experience difficulty thinking of dialogue with nature or spirit because neither appears to have a discernable linguistic language. On the other hand, when I meet another human being, I am able to enter into what Buber called *das Zwischen-menschliche*—the "interhuman"—through the realm of speech. The nature and content of language create a barrier to human interaction with nonhuman beings, but Buber clearly posits that dialogue is possible in all three of these spheres of relation.

Applying Buber's enumeration of these three realms of engagement, we can juxtapose the principal address of Chapter 1 with the principal address of Chapter 2 to form a structural grid that is essential to the structure of *I and Thou*. This Generating Grid, which will be expanded later in this chapter, demonstrates that both *I-Thou* and *I-It* occur alongside each other, often a hairsbreadth apart. Interacting both vertically and horizontally, it also reminds us that *I-Thou* relationships forever devolve into *I-It* relations, while *I-It* relations may sometimes, through grace, become *I-Thou* relationships.

The *I and Thou* Grid

REALMS	*I-THOU*	*I-IT*
With **Nature** Beneath Speech	Tree As *Thou*	Tree As *It*
With **Humans** Uses Speech	Person As *Thou*	Person As *It*
With **Spirit** **Becoming Forms** Begets Speech	Art As *Thou*	Art As *It*

Person and Nature

Having briefly distinguished the three relational realms, let us now consider some examples, first, of the relation with nature, with what Buber called "the bestowing side of things." Here, relation is not with nature as a whole but with specific and particular animals, plants, rocks, or elements. Needless to say, this relationship with both animate and inanimate nature takes place on a different level from human speech. The saying of *Thou* in this realm is a wordless saying.

At the same time, a genuine relationship with nature is direct, exclusive, and reciprocal as the other *I-Thou* relationships are. I address myself to one being alone. When I say *Thou* to a tree, for example, I am immediately present to its whole unique self, which is also present with, and to, me. Thus, for Buber, being "bound up in relation" with a tree, being wrapped up within the environment in which the tree lives, means "being seized by the power of exclusiveness" or immediate and direct unmediated relationship with another (Smith, 7). Buber writes:

SMITH, 7–8
NATURE, WILL, AND GRACE

I consider a tree.

I can look on it as a picture....

I can perceive it as movement....

I can classify it in a species and study it....

I can subdue its actual presence and form so sternly that I recognize it only as an expression of law....

I can dissipate it and perpetuate it in number....

In all this the tree remains my object, occupies space and time, and has its nature and constitution.

It can, however, also come about, if I have both will and grace, that in considering the tree I become bound up in relation to it. The tree is now no longer *It*. I have been seized by the power of exclusiveness.

KAUFMANN, 57–58
NATURE, WILL, AND GRACE

I contemplate a tree.

I can accept it as a picture....

I can feel it as movement....

I can assign it to a species and observe it....

I can overcome its uniqueness and form so rigorously that I recognize it only as an expression of the law....

I can dissolve it into a number....

Throughout all of this the tree remains my object and has its place and its time span, its kind and condition.

But it can also happen, if will and grace are joined, that as I contemplate the tree I am drawn into a relation, and the tree ceases to be an It. The power of exclusiveness has seized me.

That is, *this* tree is really a *Thou-tree*.

Although a tree lacks spontaneous verbal expression, Buber writes, "something lights up and approaches us from the course of [its] being" (Smith, 126). That is, the whole and unique reality of the tree discloses itself. It is as if the tree waits to turn green for me, and I say, "So, it is *you*." I am affected by the "*Thou*-ness" of this particular tree. It "speaks" to me without language and asks for a genuine response.

Buber continues:

SMITH, 7–8
RELATION IS MUTUAL

Everything belonging to the tree is in this: its form and structure, its colours and chemical composition, its intercourse with the elements and with the stars, are all present in a single whole.

The tree is no impression, no play of my imagination, no value depending on my mood; but it is bodied over against me and has to do with me, as I with it— only in a different way.

Let no attempt be made to sap the strength from the meaning of the relation: relation is mutual.

KAUFMANN, 58
RELATION IS RECIPROCITY

Whatever belongs to the tree is included: its form and its mechanics, its colors and its chemistry, its conversation with the elements and its conversation with the stars —all this in its entirety.

The tree is no impression, no play of my imagination, no aspect of a mood; it confronts me bodily and has to deal with me as I must deal with it—only differently.

One should not try to dilute the meaning of the relation: relation is reciprocity.

When the relationship between the tree and myself is mutual (existing from both sides) and reciprocal (giving from both sides), whatever belongs to the tree (its form and mechanics, its color and chemistry, and its natural context) discloses itself. To further explain these lines, notice what Buber later added in his "Postscript":

SMITH, 126
LIVING WHOLENESS

That living wholeness and unity of the tree, which denies itself to the sharpest glance of the mere investigator and discloses itself to the glance to the one who says *Thou,* is there when he, the sayer of *Thou,* is there: it is he who vouchsafes to the tree that it manifest this unity and wholeness: and now the tree which is in being manifests them.

KAUFMANN, 174
LIVING WHOLENESS

The living wholeness and unity of a tree that denies itself to the eye, no matter how keen, of anyone who merely investigates, while it is manifest to those who say You, is present when *they* are present: they grant the tree the opportunity to manifest it, and now the tree that has being manifests it.

In other words, during the *I-Thou* relationship the unique wholeness of one tree bestows itself. Despite our habits of thought, which make it difficult for us to "hear" it, the unique particularity of the tree nevertheless "speaks."

Practical Cats

Buber once told Maurice Friedman that if he were to write *I and Thou* again, he would try to find other language to describe the relationship with nature. There cannot be an *I-Thou,* for example, in the sense that a cat is an "I" perceiving me as a *Thou.* Nonetheless, for Buber, the cat has its own "something"—what Buber called "the bestowing side of things"—that can and does come to meet me in some sense. Buber writes:

SMITH, 97
"SPEAKING" GLANCE

Sometimes I look into a cat's eyes. The domesticated animal has not as it were received from us (as we sometimes imagine) the gift of the truly

KAUFMANN, 145
"ELOQUENT" GLANCE

I sometimes look into the eyes of a house cat. The domesticated animal has not by any means received the gift of the truly "eloquent" glance "speaking" glance, but only— at the price of its primitive disinterestedness—the capacity to turn its glance to us prodigious beings. But with this capacity there enters the glance, in its dawn and continuing in its rising, a quality of amazement and of inquiry that is wholly lacking in the original glance with all its anxiety. The beginning of this cat's glance, lighting up under the touch of my glance, indisputably questioned me: "It is possible that you think of me?...The animal's glance, speech of disquietude, rose in its greatness—and set at once. My own glance was certainly more lasting; but it was no longer the streaming human glance.

from *us,* as a human conceit suggests sometimes; what it has from us is only the ability—purchased with the loss of its elementary naturalness—to turn this glance upon us brutes. In this process some mixture of surprise and question has come into it, into its dawn and even its rise—and this was surely wholly absent from the original glance, for all its anxiety. Undeniably, this cat began its glance by asking me with a glance that was ignited by the breath of my glance: "Can it be that you mean me?...There the glance of the animal, the language of anxiety, had risen hugely— and set almost at once. My glance, to be sure, endured longer; but it no longer retained the flood of man's glance.

Of the two translations, Smith's translation is more accurate here. While the cat does not speak human language, it does speak the language of a glance, an eloquent, speaking glance. We can "hear" this "speaking" when we gaze directly into the eyes of a cat sitting on the edge of a windowsill. Suddenly, we become aware that the cat is watching us, as if it has left its world behind and entered into ours. And we might feel, too, as if we have left our world and entered the world of the cat. In response to the cat's "truly speaking glance" we are touched by the cat's unique wholeness. And in the process, our glance is altered by the cat's glance. Buber's own glance, he writes, "was no longer the streaming human glance" (Smith, 97).

A humorous and somewhat delightful analogue to Buber's *I-Thou* relationship with nature is found in T. S. Eliot's collection of poems about cats. These amusing lyrics pay tribute, for example, to "Mr. Mistoffelees," "The Rum Tum Tugger," "Macavity: The Mystery Cat," and nine other cats. Eliot's names and descriptions for cats emerge from the poet's ability to make the uniqueness of each cat present on his side of relationship. Clearly, these poems are animated by a person who genuinely loves cats. Eliot, whom Buber once met, collected these poems in *Old Possum's Book of Practical Cats.*

After introducing twelve distinctive cats, Eliot continues with "The Ad-dressing of Cats." The poem asks an italicized question: *How would you ad-dress a Cat?* Perhaps Eliot divides the word "address" into "ad-dress" to capture the directional meaning of the prefix *ad,* meaning "toward." How do we move, in other words, toward a meeting between person and person, or in this case, between person and cat? We learn from this poem, as Eliot imagines a cat's perspective, that "a Cat's entitled to expect/These evidences of respect." Without "evidences of respect" for one another, genuine relationship cannot occur. The psychotherapist Carl Rogers called this capacity for respect "unconditional personal regard."

Eliot ends the collection with a poem entitled "Cat Morgan Introduces Himself." Morgan introduces himself as a former pirate who is now retired and who can be found "a-takin' my ease." Cat Morgan concludes with a bit of advice aimed at those who are caught up in the world of business:

> You'll save yourself time, and you'll spare yourself labour
> If jist you make friends with the Cat at the door. (59)

In Buberian terms to "make friends with the Cat at the door" is analogous to being openhearted and open-minded to those whom we meet.

Person and Person

Of the three relational realms, the realm of the interhuman is the real bearer of the "between," where, for Buber, authentic human relationship occurs. Buber distinguishes this realm from the other two based on the fact that linguistic language exists on both sides of the relationship when people interact. Recall here what was said about dialogue between persons in the first chapter.

- I do not dialogue with myself, but with the other.

- Dialogue does not happen on my side of the relationship.

- The other person does not dialogue with himself or herself but with me.

- Genuine dialogue happens *between* us in a dynamic, mutual reciprocity.

By affirming that dialogue *happens,* Buber affirms that it does not occur simply by my intending it to occur. No matter how intensely I attempt to enter *I-Thou* dialogue, I cannot generate it myself. Neither can my partner. Genuine dialogue happens by virtue of relational grace, which arises from and generates the spirit of genuine meeting (we might add here: *involving spoken language*). Unmistakably pointing to the heart of Chapter 2, in the "Postscript" Buber writes:

SMITH, 135
GROUND AND MEANING

This ground and meaning of our existence constitutes a mutuality, arising again and again, such as can subsist only between persons.

KAUFMANN, 181
GROUND AND MEANING

This ground and meaning of our existence establishes each time a mutuality of the kind that can obtain only between persons.

Recall, in this context, that "all real living is meeting." Individuation is not the goal but only an indispensable way to the goal of genuine dialogue. This point is absolutely central to Buber's thought—it cannot be emphasized too strongly. Many psychotherapists and psychologists view mutual relations largely as the function and means of becoming an individual. If dialogue is entered *merely* as a means to an end (for example, maturity, self-expression, or peace of mind), it will cease to be true dialogue.

In 1914, for instance, Buber and seven other intellectual leaders from Europe met in Potsdam, Germany. Their meeting stands out in contrast to an individualistic approach to meaning. The purpose of their meeting was to attempt to find a common ground that might bring leaders of several nations together to avert the impending catastrophe of World War I. The conversations were so frank, so open-minded, and so fruitful that Buber traced his mature understanding of dialogue to exchanges among members of this group. Even though they were not successful in influencing the political climate, writing about this meeting Buber remembered not like-mindedness but rather a "mutual presence."

Address and Response

It must be clear by now that what distinguishes person-to-person relationships is shared language. We "speakingly" present ourselves to others, and engage one another through speech. In Part III of *I and Thou* Buber continually returns to and focuses our attention on the significance of speech that occurs between persons:

SMITH, 102–3 SPEECH AND COUNTER-SPEECH	KAUFMANN, 151 SPEECH AND REPLY
Of the three spheres, one, our life with men, is marked out. Here language is consummated as a sequence in speech and in counter-speech. Here alone does the word that is formed in language meet its response. Only here does the primary word go backwards and forwards in the same form, the word of address and the word of response live in the one language, *I* and *Thou* take their stand not merely in relation, but also in the solid give-and-take of talk. The moments of relation are here, and only here, bound together by means of the element of the	Of these three spheres one is distinguished: life with men. Here language is perfected as a sequence and becomes speech and reply. Only here does the word, formed in language, encounter its reply. Only here does the basic word go back and forth in the same shape; that of the address and that of the reply are alive in the same tongue; I and You do not only stand in a relationship but also in firm honesty. The moments of relation are joined here, and only here, through the element of language in which they are immersed. Here that which confronts us

speech in which they are immersed. Here what confronts us has blossomed of the full reality of the *Thou*. Here alone, then, as reality that cannot be lost, are gazing and being gazed upon, knowing and being known, loving and being loved. has developed the full actuality of the You. Here alone beholding and being beheld, recognizing and being recognized, loving and being loved exist as an actuality that cannot be lost.

The basic formal expression of the interhuman realm, according to Buber, is "address and response." Speech without meaning, and meaning without speech, are equally inconceivable in this realm. In our waking togetherness we build what Buber calls "speech-with-meaning." We enter personal relationships "through the solid give-and-take of talk."

"Here alone," Buber writes, "each person beholds and is beheld, recognizes and is recognized, loves and is loved." And most significantly, this type of relationship cannot be lost. As Friedman notes in *Encounter on the Narrow Ridge,* Lambert Schneider (who encouraged Buber to make a new translation of the Hebrew Bible into German) wrote: "What it is to listen and to answer I know since that first meeting with Martin Buber" (165).

Theatrical Dialogues

In a 1925 fragment, "Drama and Theater" (included in *Pointing the Way*), Buber wrote that drama originates and is grounded in the elemental impulse to communicate across barriers through speaking—"to leap through transformation over the abyss between *I* and *Thou* that is bridged through speech."

> Drama is therefore the formation of the *word* as something that moves *between beings,* the mystery of word and answer. Essential to it is the fact of the *tension* between word and answer; the fact, namely, that two men never mean the same things by the words that they use; that there is, therefore, no pure reply; that at each point of the conversation, therefore, understanding and misunderstanding are interwoven; from which comes then the interplay of openness and closedness, expression and reserve. (63)

The theater dramatized for Buber living tensions among various actors speaking their characters, as well as between understanding and misunderstanding, openness and closedness, expression and reserve. In Buber's story "Vienna," he spoke of the theater more intimately: "It was the word, the 'rightly' spoken human word that I received into myself, in this most real sense."

What affected Buber most strongly in the theater was the true actuality of the spirit "between." "Spirit" always remained a central part of Buber's life work. In *I and Thou*, "spirit" *(Geist)* is named as an essential element of person-with-person meetings. In the beginning of Part II, for instance, Buber suggests that the "component" of interpersonal relationship that often remains hidden, or goes unnoticed, is "spirit." Spirit, called in the King James Bible "the breath of life," is closely related to spoken language, address and response. It is the very breath required for spoken language to work.

In the following passage Buber speaks of creatively responding to another person—through ideas, through art, and through pure action—by virtue of "spirit." In its human manifestation, "spirit" animates the quality of our responses to others. After noting that a person "takes his stand in speech" (Smith, 39), that a person "stands in language and speaks out of it" (Kaufmann, 89), Buber writes:

SMITH, 39
SPIRIT

Spirit is not in the *I* but between *I* and *Thou*. It is not like the blood that circulates in you, but like the air in which you breathe. Man lives in the spirit, if he is able to respond to his *Thou*. He is able to, if he enters into relation with his whole being. Only in virtue of his power to enter into relation is he able to live in the spirit.

KAUFMANN, 89
SPIRIT

Spirit is not in the I, but between I and You. It is not like the blood that circulates in you but like the air in which you breathe. Man lives in the spirit when he is able to respond to his You. He is able to do that when he enters into this relation with his whole being. It is solely by virtue of his power to relate that man is able to live in the spirit.

Analogous to grace (indeed the very expression of grace), "spirit" exists primarily between persons, and then, within persons. Indeed, according to Buber, "spirit" generates the energy of pure relationships. Not like blood, but like the air one breathes, spirit emerges from the living situation. In that sense, "spirit" cannot become less than uniquely present.

Person and Spirit Becoming Forms

The most difficult of the three relational realms to understand is the third, *geistige Wesenheiten,* the realm translated by Smith in his first edition of *I and Thou* as "intelligible forms," and in his second edition as "spiritual beings." Kaufmann follows the second edition's precedent but, unfortunately, this translation is misleading. The third realm of relationship has nothing to do with the spiritual, as we ordinarily think of it. Rather, for Buber, *geistige Wesenheiten* relates more to meeting that which is not material. Artists meet "something," for example, and then give form to what they have met without being able materially to represent exactly that which was met.

Attempting to correct mistranslations of *geistige Wesenheiten,* Friedman suggests the phrase "intelligible essences." *Intelligible* is problematic, though, because it carries with it the connotation of "intellect," which restricts what Buber had in mind. Another interpreter, Robert Wood, suggests "forms of the spirit." While Wood's translation is closer to Buber's intention, let us look at what Buber himself has said about this term. And in a 1967 book titled simply *Martin Buber,* Ronald Gregor Smith mentions that Buber told him in a letter that the term *geistige Wesenheiten* means "spirit in phenomenal form" (16).

Perhaps "spirit becoming forms" serves better to preserve Buber's dynamic emphasis on change and plurality. Of course, the phrase "spirit becoming forms" is a bit of an oxymoron because we assume that "spirit" is formless. Certainly, this reinterpretive translation does not refer to forms that exist in a spirit world. More accurately, "spirit becoming forms" means "spirit *coming into* form"; that is, "spirit" forms and takes form through an artist's creativity, for example, or in a person's pure activity without arbitrariness, or in poetic language.

Consider, by comparison, the story of "The Woodcarver" in Thomas Merton's *The Way of Chaung Tzu* (XIX.10). In the story, Khing, a master carver, makes a bell stand from precious wood. Those who see it are amazed. "It must be the work of spirits," they say. "What is your secret?" "There is no secret," Khing replies, and tells them that he fasted for seven days in order to forget himself and to become "collected in the single thought of the bell stand." In this condition, Khing went to the forest, whereupon the bell stand appeared in exactly the right tree, beyond any doubt. Merton casts Khing's conclusion in five lines:

> "What happened?
> My own collected thought
> Encountered the hidden potential in the wood;
> From this live encounter came the work
> Which you ascribe to the spirits." (111)

"Spirit forms" come into existence only when the "collected" or creative person has a "live encounter" with them.

Regions of Spirit

Since "spirit becoming forms" implies a double meaning—both spirit in the process of forming, and the forms spirit takes—it is helpful to be aware of three interrelated regions through which, for Buber, spirit takes form in the physical world. In his "Postscript," Buber distinguishes between "spirit" that has entered the world and can be perceived, and "spirit" that has not yet entered the world, yet is ready to do so. Buber then provides two examples of "spirit becoming forms." The first, the traditional sayings of an ancient master, we discussed in the Introduction. Buber's point in this example is that the spokenness of a text can become a *Thou*. When we are fully attentive, the reader can hear a voice speaking from the text as *Thou,* speaking with an "indivisible wholeness."

Here we focus on a second example in which Buber deals with the plastic, or the solid, arts. He speaks of a powerful memory of standing before a church wall:

SMITH, 128–29
DORIC PILLAR

Out of a church wall in Syracuse, in which it had once been immured, it first came to encounter me: mysterious primal mass represented in such simple form that there was nothing individual to look out, nothing individual to enjoy. All that could be done was what I did: took my stand, stood fast, in face of this structure of spirit, this mass penetrated and given body by the mind and hand of man. Does the concept of mutuality vanish here? It only plunges back into the dark, or it is transformed into a concrete content which coldly declines to assume conceptual form, but is bright and reliable.

KAUFMANN, 175
DORIC COLUMN

It confronted me for the first time out of a church wall in Syracuse into which it had been incorporated: secret primal measure presenting itself in such a simple form that nothing individual could be seen or enjoyed in it. What had to be achieved was what I was able to achieve: to confront and endure this spiritual form there that had passed through the mind and hand of man and become incarnate. Does the concept of mutuality disappear here? It merely merges into the darkness behind it—or it changes into a concrete state of affairs, coldly rejecting concepthood, but bright and reliable.

In this remarkable event Buber feels himself addressed by a unique presence beyond words. More than the sum of its qualities (color, texture, setting), the *suchness,* the *thatness* of the Doric pillar addressed him with a full presence that could not be detached from the meeting itself. In response he could only stand firm over against the unique wholeness of this "structure of spirit." Was mutuality present there? Yes, but it remained within the realm of "spirit."[2] The mutuality of this meeting did not come from the pillar itself, but from the "spirit becoming form" embodied in the pillar's presence.

It is important to remember here that the "spirit becoming forms" are embodied but are not themselves bodies. In this passage Buber deals only with one form, the form of a certain kind of art, but in other writings he indicates two more areas in which "spirit" is realized. As mentioned above, "spirit becoming forms" implies a double meaning—both "spirit" in the process of forming, and the "forms" spirit takes. Thus it is helpful to be aware of the three interrelated regions through which spirit, in *I and Thou*, takes form: in art, ideas, and pure effective action.

The Fourth Realm

In other contexts than *I and Thou,* Buber's philosophy is suggestive of a fourth realm outside of the triad of nature, human, and spirit dialogues. In a 1938 essay, "What Is Man?" Buber speaks of this other realm:

> [A man's] threefold living relation is, first, his relation to the world and to things, second, his relation to men—both to individuals and to the many—third, his relation to the [endless transcending] mystery of being—which is dimly apparent through all of this but infinitely transcends it—what the philosopher calls the Absolute and the believer calls God, and which cannot in fact be eliminated from the situation even by a man who rejects both designations. (177)

In this passage spirit becoming forms is not mentioned as one of the three realms. Instead, Buber indicates a realm that he calls the "mystery of being"—that is, the Absolute, or God. We noted in the last chapter that, for Buber, in each interhuman address "we address the eternal *Thou*" (Smith, 6, 101).

Here, instead of speaking of spirit becoming forms, Buber speaks directly of the "eternal *Thou.*" In the "Postscript" Buber corrects the omission of this fourth realm from *I and Thou* and also switches the order of "human beings" and "spirit." The fourth realm of direct and personal dialogue, in Buber's final analysis, includes the presence of God, though not as a concept. The "eternal *Thou*," Buber implies, cannot only be related to through dialogue but can become the direct partner in the dialogue itself, as in prayer. The primary relational realms, then, are fourfold (in the order mentioned):

I AND THOU (1923)	"POSTSCRIPT" (1958)
With Nature	With Nature
With Humans	With Spirit Becoming Forms
With Spirit Becoming Forms	With Humans
	With the Eternal *Thou*

Of course, we need to recall that for Buber the "eternal *Thou*" appears, albeit dimly, through each of the other three realms when relationship is genuine. The relationship between person and person is a "real simile of the relation[ship] with God" (Smith, 103), or "proper metaphor for the relation[ship] to God" (Kaufmann, 151).

Person and the "Eternal *Thou*"

Along with nature, persons, and spirit becoming forms, one can also enter a direct relationship with the "eternal *Thou*." Very briefly here, because we will return to this subject in Chapter 5, it is useful to summarize what Buber says in the "Postscript" about meeting God:

- God is a Person in relationship with us.

- God enters into direct relationship with us in creative, revealing, redeeming acts.

- By relating to God, I bring all the other relational realms into God's relational realm and allow them to be transformed in God's presence.

- In event upon event, the personal address of God enables and empowers my ability to (1) take a stand, (2) make a decision, and (3) bear witness.

Based on the "Postscript" and Buber's description of the relational realms in "What Is Man?" we need to expand the *I and Thou* grid that opened this chapter and include the "eternal *Thou*." This inclusion is especially important because of the significance of this organizational structure for understanding Buber's thought. Since all human *Thous* become *It,* Buber can now speak of humans becoming responsible to the "eternal *Thou*," beginninglessly and endlessly.

REALMS	*I-THOU*	*I-IT*
With **Nature** Beneath Speech	Tree As *Thou*	Tree As *It*
With **Spirit** **Becoming Forms** Begets Speech	Art As *Thou*	Art As *It*
With **Humans** Uses Speech	Person As *Thou*	Person As *It*
With the **"Eternal** ***Thou***" Penetrates Speech	God As *Thou*	

Notice the radical difference between the fourth relational realm and the first three: of God, no objective aspects can be obtained. The overwhelming significance of this fourth realm, as the above figure indicates, is that God never becomes an *It.* In *Philosophical Interrogations* Buber notes:

> *In our experience* our relation to God does *not* include our I-It relations. What is the case beyond our experience, thus, so to speak, from the side of God, no longer belongs to what can be discussed. (83)

Whereas our relations with nature, persons, and spirit becoming forms can take either an *I-Thou* or *I-It* expression, our relationship to the "eternal *Thou*" can only take the *I-Thou* form. God can never become an *It,* because when God becomes a thing, or an object of experience, or a doctrine to be believed, the living God is lost in the thought of the living God. For Buber, the "eternal *Thou*" is always "wholly Present," inviting us into deeper relationships, even though we continue trying to relate to God as a theological concept, or a gender, or a philosophical being.

Meetings

To help take us more deeply into Buber's understanding of the relational realms in connection with the two primal word pairs, we conclude with an anecdote from *Meetings* in which Buber tells a childhood tale of a horse. What follows is an attention-grabbing narration of a young boy's self-discovery coming as a result of his *I-Thou* relationship, which then devolves into an experience of self-reflexive enjoyment. In it, Buber discovered the difference between a genuine *I-Thou* relationship and a partial, *I-It* relation.

The Horse

When I was eleven years of age, spending the summer on my grandparents' estate, I used, as often as I could do it unobserved, to steal into the stable and gently stroke the neck of my darling, a broad dapple-gray horse. It was not a casual delight but a great, certainly friendly, but also deeply stirring happening. If I am to explain it now, beginning from the still very fresh memory of my hand, I must say that what I experienced in touch with the animal was the Other, the immense otherness of the Other, which, however, did not remain strange like the otherness of the ox and the ram, but rather let me draw near and touch it. When I stroked the mighty mane, sometimes marvelously smooth-combed, at other times just as astonishingly wild, and felt the life beneath my hand, it was as though the element of vitality itself bordered on my skin, something that was not I, was certainly not akin to me, palpably the other, not just another, really the Other itself; and yet it let me approach, confided itself to me, placed itself elementally in the relation of *Thou* and *Thou* with me. The horse, even when I had not begun by pouring oats for him into the manger, very gently raised his massive head, ears flicking, then snorted quietly, as a conspirator gives a signal meant to be recognizable only by his fellow-conspirator; and I was approved. But once—I do not know what came over the child, at any rate it was childlike enough—it struck me about the stroking, what fun it gave me, and suddenly I became conscious of my hand. The game went on as before, but something had changed, it was no longer the same thing. And the next day, after giving him a rich feed, when I stroked my friend's head he did not raise his head. A few years later, when I thought back to the incident, I no longer supposed that the animal had noticed my defection. But at the time I considered myself judged. (26–27)

In Buber's meeting with the dapple-gray horse, the difference between an *I-Thou* relationship and an *I-It* relation is reflected. As long as the young Buber turned fully toward the horse, the animal became a vital other in a relationship of "*Thou* and *Thou*"—a "fellow-conspirator." Indeed, Buber felt that the horse approved of him by snorting a quiet signal meant only for him. Once Buber became aware of the fun he was having while stroking the horse, though, he became self-conscious, and conscious of the horse as an object of his perception. At that point, something shifted. The genuine dialogue between them ceased. The horse no longer lifted its head when Buber stroked it. And Buber felt judged.

Practice Exercises

In dialogue circles and in your dialogue journal, practice with the ideas of this chapter by responding to some of these questions.

1. With whom do I choose to enter dialogue, if anyone, if ever?

2. Ponder and comment on the following:

   • How are the four realms relevant to your life?

   • What are the most significant differences among the four realms?

   • Have you ever talked to a plant? What did you say, and did it answer?

3. Think of a place around your neighborhood where you can be in nature. It may be on a hiking trial in the woods or a long stretch of sandy beach. Take a tape recorder or a journal and go there with the thought of communicating about what you meet. Try not to think of nature as just vegetation; look past the places of physical confinement. Try to see the distances between earth and clouds, clouds and sky, sky and space, for example. Remember that whether you are looking upward at the stars or downward at the earth, you can be met by the unique particularity of an element in nature without speech. Share your responses with the members in your learning community.

4. Form groups of two. Share a dialogical event with your partner. Remember that sharing the experience does not have to be perfect. Verbal expressions of nonverbal events are difficult to convey, so transmitting your experience may take some creative "human" examples. Either way, be patient and do not judge whether you are being understood. Share your story with the members in your learning community.

5. Think of an event in which you responded to art, or architecture, or music. At the moment of meeting and being met by the other, what type of communication occurred? Or think about an event in which you suddenly had a great idea that impelled you to form, paint, or generate

something very creative. Perhaps it was a dance, a letter, a painting, or a collage that means a lot to you. Thinking about the event afterward, how did you feel during it, and how did you feel after it was completed?

6. After sharing your responses with the group, you may wish to dialogue with your journal. You may also wish to record what others have said in response to your account of the event. In what ways did their voices assist you to come to a deeper understanding of the event?

Notes

1. In a series of lectures entitled "Religion as Presence," presented in 1922 just prior to the publication of *I and Thou* (included in Rivka Horwitz's *Buber's Way to "I and Thou"*), Buber elaborated the moment of authentic meeting in urgent language. It is worth repeating that language here because it helps clarify Buber's intention:

> The truth and importance of the event is that something happens to us; we receive something we did not have before, and we receive it in such a way that we know with our innermost being that something has been given to us. All attempts at interpretation are infinitely weaker, are infinitely vain, in the face of this immensely important event. (114–15)

2. It is appropriate to wonder if all these three relationships (with nature, with persons, and with spirit becoming forms) have anything in common. In Buber's 1922 lecture series entitled "Religion as Presence," he succinctly addressed this question:

> By entering into a relationship with [nature, persons, spirit becoming forms] I do not make it an experience; rather, I make it an actuality, a presence, or, to put it more correctly, it becomes a presence for me, through me, in confrontation with me. (65)

Notice Buber's shift from "I make it an actuality" to "it becomes a presence for me." Genuine relationships happen through no self-directed, self-contained intention.

PART II

GENUINE RELATIONSHIPS

Spirit is not in the *I*, but between *I* and *Thou*.
It is not like the blood that circulates in you,
but like the air in which you breathe.
 —MARTIN BUBER, *I and Thou* (Smith, 39)

Chapter 3

What Is "Genuine Community"?

> The true community does not arise through peoples
> having feelings for one another (though indeed not without
> it), but through, first, their taking their stand in living
> mutual relation with a living Centre, and, second, their
> being in living mutual relation with one another.

In Chapters 1 and 2, we focused our attention on the *I and Thou* grid, which grounds Buber's *I-Thou* philosophy and especially describes his vision of human communication in the world. We discussed the basic axis of Buber's thought: *I-Thou* and *I-It,* overlaid with the relational realms of nature, of persons, of spirit becoming forms, and of the "eternal *Thou.*" Part II of Buber's *I and Thou* distinguishes itself by providing two behavioral consequences of Part I's fundamental premises. In Chapters 3 and 4, therefore, we will study, ponder, and practice two dialogically reciprocal, person-with-person relationships that emerge from Part I.

Part II of *I and Thou* opens by articulating and emphasizing components of the *It*-world, and then shifts focus to provide two social expressions of the *I-Thou* relationship—through community, and through personal wholeness. Buber's social philosophy mainly describes both historical-social-institutional experiences of human life, but it also sets out to describe authentic personal human behavior. Thus, in Chapter 3 we consider and reflect upon "genuine community"; in Chapter 4 we turn the discussion toward what Buber calls the "real *I*."

The World of *It*

Buber ended Part I of *I and Thou* by asserting that the world of *It* is necessary for human life but—and this remains Buber's caveat throughout—one who lives continuously and exclusively in the world of *It* does not become fully human. Buber begins Part II of *I and Thou* with a further elaboration of the *It*-world, of our ever-expanding capacity "to experience," "to use," and "to know."

The history of the individual and that of the human race, Buber suggests, are marked by a progressive domination of humankind over the world of things. Our basic connection to this world encompasses both experiencing and using in various combinations. As our sense of the world of things expands, the capacity to experience and to use also increases. These capacities develop from generation to generation. Succinctly, Buber writes: "The development of the function of experiencing and using is obtained mostly through a reduction of the power of relation[ship]" (Smith, 45). Quite clearly, then, an ability to function well in the world of *It* can reduce a person's ability to commune in the world of *I and Thou.*

When human life becomes a function of experiencing and using, it tends to divide consciousness artificially into two regions: the region of institutions, and the region of feelings. The first is societal and includes the worlds of organized industry and government. The second is personal and includes the world of likes, pleasures, and pains. Institutions mostly deal with objects and are therefore much less interested in the wholeness of the human person. Feelings, though, are mostly subjective and do not encompass the wholeness of true relationship.

In a time when a collective society's ability to function well in the rubric of *I-It* relations has become gigantically swollen, it becomes more and more difficult for individuals to suspend the perception of everyone and everything as an object for personal consumption or gratification. Buber writes:

SMITH, 48–49
NATURAL AND PROPER

The communal life of man can no more than man himself dispense with the world of *It,* over which the presence of *Thou* moves like the spirit upon the face of the waters. Man's will to profit and [his will] to be powerful have their natural and proper effect so long as they are linked with, and upheld by, his will to enter into relation. There is no evil impulse till the impulse has been separated from the being; the impulse which is bound up with, and defined by, the being is the living stuff of communal life, that which is detached is its disintegration. Economics, the abode of the will to profit, and State, the abode of the will to be powerful, share in life as long as they share in the spirit.

KAUFMANN, 97–98
NATURAL AND LEGITIMATE

Man's communal life cannot dispense any more than he himself, with the It-world—over which the presence of the You floats like the spirit over the face of the waters. Man's will to profit and will to power are natural and legitimate as long as they are tied to the will to human relations and carried by it. There is no evil drive until the drive detaches itself from our being; the drive that is wedded to and determined by our being is the plasma of communal life, while the detached drive spells its disintegration. The economy as the house of the will to profit and the state as the house of the will to power participate in life as long as they participate in the spirit.

Certainly, Buber is not rejecting the world of *It.* He understands that experiencing, using, and knowing affects everything we do. However, with the accumulated thickening of *I-It* related behaviors, such reifying activity tends to become detrimentally habitual. *It*-oriented activity strikes inwardly so powerfully that we are left with severely diminished capacities to express our unique wholeness or to affirm that of another. Indeed, as Buber writes, the "inborn *Thou*" recedes. We become trapped within ourselves.

While we cannot dispense with the world of *It,* our drive to profit and be powerful needs direction from the presence of *I-Thou* relationships. It is these authentic relationships that prevent the world of *It* from overtaking us and that introduce ultimate meaning and intrinsic value into life. Buber, living at the peak of the Industrial Revolution and through two world wars, was keenly aware of the dangers of object-oriented consciousness. No doubt, Buber would have spoken differently along these lines in today's information-oriented environment, in which ideas are treated as temporary and dispensable objects for personal consumption and power. Though our object-orientation has shifted somewhat, the basic *I-It* attitude remains as prevalent as it ever was.

The basic limitation with the world of *It* for Buber, the reason that *I-It* relations fail to support interhuman life, is that "the other," a *"Thou"* by birthright, becomes gradually reduced to an object of feelings. How one relates to another person is determined, then, more by how one *feels* about them and less by how they actually are. Has the other treated me the way I want/need to be treated? Can I profit from acting in a certain manner toward the other? Do I like/appreciate the way the other looks? Answers to questions like these restrict our willingness to be fully present.

The "Essential We"

When personal lives become feeling-oriented, when emotions dominate us to the point of determining our life attitudes, it becomes difficult to realize that personal feelings by themselves yield no interhuman life. Missing from a life of mere feelings is what Buber calls the "essential we"—*I-Thou* relationships built up in community. Genuine community cannot be based on how one feels about another or about some thing. Instead, authentic community—the "essential we"—is built upon readiness in every moment to enter living relationships.

- The relation between persons takes place not only in the *I-Thou* relationship of direct meeting but also in the "we" of community.

- As the primitive *Thou* precedes the essential *Thou,* the primitive we precedes the "essential we."

- The "essential we" occurs when independent people come together in direct relationship to one another.

- The "essential we" includes those who are capable of truly saying *Thou* to one another.

- The "essential we" must be continually renewed through the interplay of genuine dialogues.

To begin to understand what Buber means by genuine community, it is important to understand what he does not mean. For one thing, genuine community can never exclusively mean, for Buber, collectivity, or institutionalized social relations. Collectivity is based on an organized union of forces; community, on the other hand, is based on life lived in communion with one another. Collectivity tends toward quantity and sameness—psychological mass production—which, for Buber, limits the meaning-oriented dialogue true community enables. A collection of individuals pursuing common interests, needs, or appetites usually does not allow for uniquely transforming meetings to occur.

Buber frequently employed the term *Gemeinschaft* for "community." *Gemeinschaft* refers to the "vital interaction" between complete and thoroughly responsive persons who are just as content giving as taking. *Gemeinschaft,* referred to by Buber in a 1919 essay of that name, means a "stream of giving and creative surrender." According to Buber, true community cannot be set forth as a goal to be obtained; rather, it arises when people learn to really listen to one another again. *by product*

It is helpful here to recall that thirty years after publishing *I and Thou,* in one of his most important philosophical essays, "Elements of the Interhuman" (in *The Knowledge of Man*), Buber clarified what he meant by genuine dialogue. In a section entitled "Genuine Dialogue," Buber writes that central to "I-Thou" dialogue are not two, but three elements: (1) the dialogical person *("I")*, (2) the unique other *("Thou")*, and (3) the "between" *(Zwischen)*. For Buber, one becomes fully human in the relationship with the other (whether nature, human, or spirit becoming forms) through elemental togetherness. To understand Buber's use of "genuine community," it is crucial, therefore, to consider how

Buber describes these reciprocal mutualities, especially "the between."

The Between

Not fully described until after *I and Thou,* the realm of "the between" is yet absolutely essential to all of Buber's dialogical philosophy. The interhuman *(das Zwischenmenschliche)* is generated by the immediate presence that binds together a conscious "self" with a conscious "other." In this mutual presence—common to each yet reaching out beyond either person—the innermost self of each person arises simultaneously. "The between" occurs when one turns to the other and enters into an undivided relationship. This interhuman sphere is significant because it refers to shared relationships—whether between single persons or persons in community. In *Between Man and Man,* Buber conveys a memorably new understanding of genuine dialogue in society.

> On the far side of the subjective, on this side of the objective, on the narrow ridge, where *I and Thou* meet, there is the realm of "between."…Here the genuine third alternative is indicated, the knowledge of which will help to bring about the genuine person again and to establish genuine community. (204)

More than an inner experience, or realization, or transformation, the "oscillating sphere" of "the between," as Buber said, is both ontological (referring to what is *really* real), and existential, or *concretely* present. Neither individualistic nor collectivistic, neither inner nor outer, nor the sum of the two, the interhuman realm is a "genuine third alternative" between subjectivity and objectivity. Common to each, yet reaching beyond their separateness, neither imagined nor constructed, "the between" is relational space ever and again reconstituted in our meetings with others and ever and again establishing genuine dialogue and genuine community.

In the most powerful moments of dialogue, when "deep calls unto deep," it becomes unmistakably clear that genuine relationship is not individual or social but found in the mutual presence of human relationships. In the depths of "the between," grounded in and generated by the "spirit" embodied in relationship, the mutual giving of person and person becomes immediately present. On the far side of the *"I,"* on this side of the *"Thou,"* where *I* and *Thou* meet, true community happens. Buber's philosophy of "the between" in *The Knowledge of Man* can be schematized as follows:

SELF *(I)*	THE BETWEEN (THE INTERHUMAN)	OTHER *(THOU)*
Turning Toward Others	Persons Turning Toward Each Other	As "the Single One"
Making the Other Present	Reciprocal Partners	As Unique
Including the Other	"A Memorable Common Fruitfulness"	As Personal
Accepting, Affirming, Confirming	A "Dynamic of Elemental Togetherness"	As Whole

Reciprocal Mutualities

There are two interconnected relationships, or reciprocal mutualities, embodied in every genuine dialogical community. In a key passage of *I and Thou,* Buber writes:

SMITH, 45 "LIVING EFFECTIVE CENTRE"	KAUFMANN, 94 "LIVING, ACTIVE CENTER"
The true community does not arise through peoples having feelings for one another (though indeed not without it), but through first, their taking their stand in living mutual relation with a living Centre, and, second, their being in living mutual	True community does not come into being because people have feelings for each other (though that is required, too), but rather on two accounts: all of them have to stand in a living, reciprocal relationship to a single living center, and they have to

relation with one another. The second has its source in the first, but is not given when the first alone is given. Living mutual relation includes feelings but does not originate with them. The community is built up out of living mutual relation, but the builder is the living effective Centre.

stand in a living, reciprocal relationship to one another. The second event has its source in the first but is not immediately given with it. A living reciprocal relationship includes feelings but is not derived from them. A community is built upon a living, reciprocal relationship, but the builder is the living, active center.

"True community" in this passage does not come into being through a person's feelings about another or about an issue. It involves interhuman relationships of persons mutually and reciprocally united. True community arises, in Buber's view, (1) through interactions with other members of the group; and (2) through interactions with the living center of the group that is the master builder of community.

In 1949 Buber wrote a poem for his wife, Paula, which he inscribed in her copy of *Tales of the Hasidim,* speaking lyrically to describe both genuine dialogue and genuine community as mutual give-and-take processes. Three lines from the poem especially stand out:

Each kindling each, with each one adding parts
To new descriptions, a new entity
Came into being between you and me.

The realization of the basic elements of *Gemeinschaft* by its very nature contains at least two partners. It was Buber's interaction with his wife, Paula, that directed him to understand the essential connection between genuine dialogue and genuine community. That is, what initially brings people together in genuine community is a common yearning, a longing deep within each person for relationship, a yearning Buber associates with the "inborn *Thou.*" But who is the "master builder"? What is "the *living* effective Centre" required for founding or renewing true community?

The "Central *Thou*"

Real community, in Buber's view, originates and continually renews itself as a group of people participating in and around a dialogical center. We should pause, therefore, to consider four brief passages in which Buber speaks of the living center of mutual relationship upon which true community is built. First, in Part II of *I and Thou* Buber writes:

SMITH, 46 "CENTRAL *THOU*"	KAUFMANN, 95 "CENTRAL YOU"
True public and true personal life are two forms of connexion. In that they come into being and endure, feelings (the changing content) and institutions (the constant form) are necessary; but put together they do not create human life: this is done by the third, the central presence of the *Thou,* or rather, more truly stated, by the central *Thou* that has been received in the present.	True public and true personal life are two forms of association. For them to originate and endure, feelings are required as a changing content, and institutions, are required as a constant form; but even the combination of both still does not create human life which is created only by a third element: the central presence of the You, or rather, to speak more truthfully, the central You that is received in the present.

Buber introduces here, and describes, the generative center of genuine community. The word translated by Smith as "connexion," and by Kaufmann as "association"—*Verbundenheit*—is another one of Buber's central terms; it might better be translated "deep bonding." What creates dialogical community is the central presence of *Thou,* a spirit of common mutuality specific to each group's way of bonding deeply. This bonding both generates and is generated by the community's members.

The "central *Thou*" is not a permanent entity or fixed idea but, like the "essential we," must continually be renewed. "The central *Thou*" can be understood as the group's spirit of mutuality in the form of a leader (the *zaddik* of a Hasidic community), or a common task, or a dynamic connection through which a community forms itself. A family is a living community whose "central *Thou*" includes the love members share for one another, along with the common task of maintaining healthy family relationships.[1]

Artistic communities, for instance, often thrive on dynamic and co-creative connections. Political communities, on the other hand, usually form around a leader or leadership group that personifies the community's agenda. Formations of communities vary, and new communities can grow up out of the "central *Thou*" that is called forth when separate groups engage one another genuinely.

A few pages later in Part II, Buber offers a structural description of real community life. As he does in other passages, he briefly steps away from the pages of his text and poses a question that seems to challenge his own position. "Wouldn't their world come crashing down upon them," Buber asks of the community, "if they refused to add up He+He+He to get an It, and tried instead to determine the sum of You and You and You, which can never be anything else than You?" (Kaufmann, 96). Buber acknowledges that, through it all, the machinery of the economy hums in an unwarranted manner. As this occurs, one's "I" becomes "more impotent," but dreaming that it is in control. While the will to profit and the will to power are "natural and legitimate," he warns:

SMITH, 49
POWER TO ENTER RELATION

KAUFMANN, 98
RELATIONAL FORCE

The loosening of the structure of economics or of the State cannot compensate for their being no longer under the dominance of the spirit that says *Thou:* no disturbance on the periphery can serve as substitute for the living relation with the Centre. Structures of man's communal life draw their living quality from

Loosening the framework of the economy or the state cannot make up for the fact that neither stands any longer under the supremacy of the You-saying spirit, and stirring up the periphery cannot replace the living relationship to the center. The structures of the communal human life derive their life from the fullness of the riches of the power to enter into relation, which penetrates their various parts, and obtain their bodily form from the binding up of this power in the spirit.

the relational force that permeates their members, and they derive their embodied form from the saturation of this force by the spirit.

True Human Community

Toward the end of Part III of *I and Thou* Buber returns to the theme of genuine community and evokes the metaphor of the periphery and the center. Buber almost graphically depicts an image of a circle whose radii move from the periphery (which is the community) to the center.

SMITH, 115 PERIPHERY AND RADII	KAUFMANN, 163 PERIPHERY AND RADII
The moments of supreme meeting are then not flashes in darkness but like the rising moon in a clear starlit night. Thus, too, the authentic assurance of constancy in space consists of the fact that men's relations with their true *Thou,* the radial lines proceed from all the points of the *I* to the Centre, form a circle. It is not the periphery, the community, that comes first, but the radii, the common quality of relation with the Centre. This alone guarantees the authentic existence of the community.	The moments of supreme encounter are no mere flashes of lightning in the dark, but like a rising moon in a clear starry night. And thus the genuine guarantee of spatial constancy consists in this that men's relations to their true You, being radii that lead from all I-points to the center, create a circle. Not the periphery, not the community comes first, but the radii, the common relation to the center. That alone assures the genuine existence of a community.

Clarifying his intentions here in an essay titled "Comments on the Idea of Community" (in *A Believing Humanism*), Buber writes that "community is the inner constitution of a common life that knows and embraces differences":

The real essence of community is undoubtedly to be found in the—manifest or hidden—fact that it has a center. The real origin of community is undoubtedly only to be understood by the fact that its members have a common relationship to the center superior to all other relations: the circle is drawn from the radii, not from the points of the periphery. And undoubtedly the primal reality of the center cannot be known if it is not known as transparent into the divine. (89)

Comparing these passages, it becomes clear that the power to enter into a living reciprocal relationship, according to Buber, both flows toward and reflects the "central *Thou*"—itself transparent to the divine. We can say that *I-Thou* relationships point to the center of a wheel, the periphery of which is a community of authentic human interactions. Yet what really counts is not the community as such, but living in communion that emanates along the radii from the center.

Buber's image of a true community, comprised of persons in genuine relationship with one another and with a "central *Thou*," is illustrated in Figure 3–1.

Figure 3–1

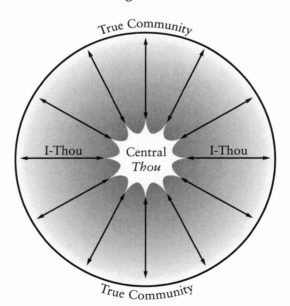

Paula

In the midst of discussing true community in *I and Thou,* Buber interjects a universal exemplification, the example of marriage. Since, for Buber, "love is responsibility of an *I* for a *Thou,*" and given that feelings are within a person while love is between *I* and *Thou,* it follows that marriage renews itself through its true origin—namely, through two persons revealing their *Thou* to each other. According to Buber, one should not confuse the *feelings* of love (which may or may not be present) with the real expression of love (which is always relational).

According to Maurice Friedman, Buber's relationship to his wife, Paula, was of crucial importance for his life's work. In the summer of 1899, while attending the University of Zurich, Buber met Paula Winkler. They married shortly after, despite objections that she was a Gentile, "a pagan," as she joked. Although raised a Munich Catholic, she converted to Judaism and in so doing lost her own family. Yet, remarkably, as Hugo Bergmann observed, when Paula said "we Jews," "we felt ourselves confirmed."

Paula was a woman given to an enormous amount of intellectual energy and physical work. Friends related, and Buber understood, that she was in many ways emotionally stronger and more mature than Buber. She possessed an impressive intellect and poetic talent, acquiring a reputation as a writer and poet under the pseudonym Georg Munk. In Paula, Martin found true equality of relationship. And with Paula, Buber came to recognize that a marriage is built upon the saying of *Thou.*

Along with Buber, Paula became an enthusiastic participant in helping to create a life of community and dialogue. In a way, Buber regained his missing mother in Paula. She lent him strength and emotional support and direction for his unharnessed creative energies. In *Martin Buber's Life and Work,* Friedman writes:

> To grasp the full significance of Buber's approach to love and marriage in *I and Thou,* we must first speak of his relationship to his wife Paula—an influence probably more decisive for his I-Thou philosophy than any of the events or meetings that we have discussed. Buber's dialogical thinking could

have grown only out of his marriage to this strong and really "other" woman, this modern Ruth who left her family, home, and religion, and finally even her country and people, for him. The fundamental reality of the life of dialogue—that is a confirmation and inclusion of otherness—was understood and authenticated in the love and the marriage, the tension and the companionship of his relationship to Paula. (1:336)

Mutual Animated Describing

While his mother's disappearance came to signify the crucial "mismeeting" of Buber's life, his marriage to Paula was the crucial "meeting"; it restored his trust in the eternal possibility of genuine relationships. One catches glimpses of Martin and Paula's relationship through their letters. Their early letters (collected in *The Letters of Martin Buber*) are intense, honest, encouraging, silly, deeply loving. On August 14, 1899, Paula wrote:

> Sweet, dear, You must not start worrying immediately when a letter does not reach you....I do earnestly ask that of you. I have fond feelings for your great work—I would never want to spoil it for but I would like to slip myself between you and the little everyday bothers, like a sheltering cloud. That is why I so wish I were with you. (66)

And on November 17, 1901, she wrote:

> Dearest Mowgli,
> Mowgli dear, you were lovable in your last little note. It has filled me with courage and joy again, dearest. Yes, of course, dear heart, I love you beyond anything. And the good days when we'll feel that properly from heart to heart, they're just beginning, my only one. (79–80)

The significance of Buber's trust in Paula's good judgment and advice is evident in a letter he wrote to her on October 25, 1901, during a spell of depression:

> Dear Heart, Your letter may well be the right answer to mine. It certainly has pushed me hard. There is one thing you

cannot understand, dearest: that every moment here I am struggling with every fiber of my being to bear up against all my restlessness, against all my cares, against all my knowledge, against all my deprivation, against everything that is trying to crush me. Every moment. And that your letters are the only source of strength for me. (79)

As these letters suggest, it was with Paula that Buber first came to realize and articulate the "mutual meeting" that characterized the spirit between them. Paula's strength, her integrity, and her responsibility are movingly celebrated in a poem that Buber wrote to her on her fiftieth birthday, "On the Day of Looking Back." Buber ends the poem with a powerful acknowledgment and confirmation of his wife:

> Then both spirit and world became open to me,
> The lies burst, and what was, was enough.
> You brought it about that I behold,—
> Brought about? you only lived.
> You element and woman,
> Soul and nature!

In a later poem, "Do You Still Know It?" Buber credits Paula with helping him find direction for his talents and interests. In it, he writes two lines that again link genuine dialogue with genuine community:

> How a mutual animated describing
> Arose out of it and lived between you and me!

The phrase "mutual animated describing" points directly to the interhuman realm of "the between," as well as to the "central *Thou*" and to the "essential we." Buber's understanding of genuine community, it seems, arose out of a lived relationship between Paula and himself. It is little wonder, then, that the epigraph with which Buber began *I and Thou* is considered a dedication to Paula as well.

> So waiting I have won from thee the end
> God's presence in each element.

The Hasidic Community

Since, for Buber, genuine community was rare, one has a right to wonder if it exists at all. And if so, when and where? Buber set out to answer this question, of course, and continuously reiterated two of his favorite examples of genuine community, each illustrating his vision for community dialogue. The first is the legendary Hasidic community, which has been handed down to us in stories and tales told by fervent souls (the Hasidim) who were members of a communal movement that sought to unite holy intent *(kavanah)* with the Divine Presence *(Shekinah)*. The second community is *educational,* whether classes, seminars, or study groups.

Buber's interest in Hasidism—the mystical movement of East European Jewry that rose to fame in the eighteenth and nineteenth centuries—was first ignited when his grandfather took him to religious services. There he witnessed the rebbe standing in silent prayer and interpreting the mystery of Torah. When he saw the Hasidim verbally dance with the Torah, he reports that he felt his strongest personal sense of community. The Hasidim embodied for Buber the living double kernel of humanity: genuine community, on the one hand, and genuine leadership, on the other. In *Philosophical Interrogations* he writes:

> The Hasidic communal group, like all genuine community, consists of men who have a common, immediate relation to a living center, and just by virtue of this common center have an immediate relation to one another. In the midst of the Hasidic community stands the *zaddik,* whose function it is to help the Hasidim, as persons and as a totality, to authenticate their relation to God in the hallowing of life. (68)

In 1904 Buber discovered *The Testament of Rabbi Israel Baal-Shem,* a collection of sayings attributed to Israel Ben Eliezer (1700–1760). He was known as the Baal-Shem-Tov, master of the good name of God, and was the founder of the Hasidim. The study of Hasidism caused something of an epiphany for Buber. He later noted that it combined a "summons" and a "sending forth" that would eventually lead to *I and Thou.*

As a movement, European Hasidism saw no division between religion and ethics, or between one's direct relation to God and one's relation to others. The true Hasid (the devout one who kept faith with the covenant) sanctified the everyday world. Each person was responsible for the piece of the world entrusted to him or her. It was this Hasidic teaching of full presence in the world and, at the same time, full presence with God that underpins the central tenets of Buber's life philosophy. But how does a person discover the divine sparks hidden in everyday reality?

According to the Hasidic tradition, one needs a helper, a counselor. This helper, for both body and soul, was called the *zaddik,* the righteous, the one who stands the test. The *zaddikim* were leaders, teachers, and tradition bearers whose authority rose from the lives they lived. If one of Buber's favorite images of genuine community is that of the Hasidim, it was because the *zaddik* stood in its midst.

In the first volume of *Tales of the Hasidim,* Buber explains the roles of the *zaddik.* The leader of the Hasidic community

- takes you by the hand and guides you until you are able to venture on alone;

- does not relieve you of doing what you have grown strong enough to do for yourself;

- strengthens the Hasid in the hours of doubting;

- develops the Hasid's power of prayer;

- teaches the Hasid how to give the words of prayer the right direction; and

- joins his own prayer to that of his community, and therewith lends it courage, and an increase of power. (4–5)

The *zaddik,* or the true helper, was for Buber the ideal example of a holy human being. The *zaddik*'s presence was an indispensable pivot, the center of a community continuously turning toward dialogue. At the same time, the dialogue between the *zaddik* and the Hasid was intertwined with each person's dialogue with God. Thus, in such a community, to come closer to one's being, one absolutely needs to enter into meaningful relationships with others. And to enter meaningful relationships with others, one needs to enter meaningful relationship with the "eternal *Thou.*"

At this point a reader may wonder about the relevance of a historic movement only coincidentally associated with modern-day Hasidism. How does it matter to today's culture? Buber would respond that European Hasidism provides us with an image of genuine community that suggests how people can transformatively participate in all types of existing communities. In other words, Hasidism provides a direction of movement, a constellation of tendencies toward genuine community that can be practiced in today's context. For Buber, the Hasidic "way" ever and again turned toward its teaching of wholeness and presence. The "wholeness" of a particular situation always involves a uniquely living relationship between persons through which the "eternal partner" is clearly seen and acknowledged.[2]

The Learning Community

Buber's second example of genuine community is the educational community—what Maurice Friedman calls the "learning community." Friedman writes that to understand the authentication of human community in society one must distinguish between two different types of community—the "community of affinity," and the "community of otherness." The community of affinity, or like-mindedness, is based on what people feel they have in common with one another (race, sex, nationality, politics, religion, and so on).

In the "community of affinity," on the other hand, inclusive people, finding themselves in a common, caring situation with others, make the community genuine. Friedman calls the community of affinity the "caring community." A genuine educational community, from this point of view, cannot be founded simply on good intentions. What brings a group of people together in meaningful ways is a living togetherness, constantly renewed among and within members. In communal interactions each person interacts with the unique wholeness of the other. An educational community, therefore, is a community of learners who mutually confirm the otherness of each person (students and teachers) within the kind of structure we call educational.

Buber's university work was dedicated to promoting adult education and teacher training. In Nazi Germany, when Jewish students had been excluded from public education, Buber led a movement to form youth groups under the direction of the teachers that his planning had helped to train. Politically, he rejected the language of tolerance or neutrality in education in favor of unfolding the roots of community through living mutual support and living mutual action. Buber envisioned a model of genuine community that he called the "community of communities."

Twelve years after publishing *I and Thou,* in a 1935 educational bulletin called "Education and World-View," he wrote that "everything depends upon how much one actually has to do with the world that one is interpreting." The decisive question about one's world view, therefore, is whether it enables one to connect more vitally to the world or obstructs that possibility. Rather than intervening between a person and the world, the goal of education should be to help one live more deeply in the world.[3]

The learning community, an ever-regenerated community of people who are willing to be *present* to and for one another, necessarily recognizes and openly discusses multiple points of view. Diversity is not a difficulty to be overcome. A learning community's multiplicity of viewpoints provides the material for ever-recurring dialogues, because each person brings something quite concrete and unique into the communal relationship. Open-minded honesty and willingness to be changed are valued more than like-mindedness. Again, it should be remembered that genuine community, for Buber, is not only an ideal but also a direction of movement, a reality that we try to build in every situation. A learning community happens through open-minded dialogue—open to otherness, and open to various points of view.

In Buber's terms, learning as genuine dialogue occurs when

- we are present with our whole being;
- we do not withhold ourselves, but communicate everything that comes to mind without being judgmental;

- we have the courage not only to address but also to respond to the other; and

- we recognize that speech-with-meaning arises in the process of building together a common situation.

Meetings

As we have in previous chapters, we conclude this chapter with an anecdote from *Meetings*. In this incident Buber speaks of his attraction to the Hasidic community:

The Zaddik

In my childhood I spent every summer on an estate in Bukovina. There my father took me with him at times to a nearby village of Sadagora. Sadagora is the seat of a dynasty of *"zaddikim"* (*zaddik* means righteous, proven), that is, of the Hasidic rabbis. There no longer lives in the present-day community that high faith of the first Hasidim, that fervent devotion which honored in the *zaddik* the perfected man in whom the immortal finds its mortal fulfillment. Rather the present-day Hasidim turn to the *zaddik* above all as the mediator through whose intercession they hope to attain the satisfaction of their needs. Even in these degenerate Hasidim there still continues to glow, in the unknown ground of their souls, the word of rabbi Eliezar that the world was created for the sake of the perfected man (the *zaddik*), even though there should be only one.

This I realized at the time, as a child, in the dirty village of Sadagora from the "dark" Hasidic crowd that I watched—as a child realizes such things, not as thought, but as image and feeling—that the world needs the perfected man and that the perfected man is none other than the true helper. Certainly, the power entrusted to him has been misinterpreted by the faithful, had been misused by himself. But is it not at base a legitimate, the legitimate power, this power of the helping soul over the needy? Does there not lie in it the seed of future social orders?

> At any rate, in a childish fashion, these questions already dawned on me at that time. And I could compare on the one side with the head man of the province whose power rested on nothing but habitual compulsion; on the other with the rabbi, who was an honest and God-fearing man, but an employee of the "directorship of the cult." Here, however, was another, an incomparable; here was, debased yet uninjured, the living double kernel of humanity: genuine *community* and genuine *leadership*.
>
> The place of the *rebbe*, in its showy splendor, repelled me. The prayer house of the Hasidim with its enraptured worshipers seemed strange to me. But when I saw the *rebbe* striding through the rows of the waiting, I felt, "leader," and when I saw the Hasidim dance with the Torah, I felt "community." At the time there rose in me a presentiment of the fact that common reverence and common joy of soul are the foundations of genuine human community. (38–39)

Consider this incident again. It is important to note that community and leader are one inseparable "living double kernel." While the kernel is one, within it is relationship. What Buber realized in the anecdote is twofold: (1) that the world needs whole persons (fully unique, united, and holy); and (2) that the world needs perfected communities. In this realization of reciprocal powers—helping and being helped—Buber located the germinating seed of new social orders.

Practice Exercises

1. What does it mean to be a member of a genuine community in which one chooses to live a life of dialogue?

2. Describe a community in which your participation most nearly coincides with the genuine dialogue that Buber has been describing. Give examples of how people relate to one another in this community.

3. Have anger and disagreement in your community ever made you fear that the group would dissolve? If it didn't dissolve, what did you do to prevent the community from falling apart? Reflecting back on the experience, what could you have done to encourage an open-minded exchange of ideas?

4. In a dialogue circle, discuss how Buber's idea of genuine community applies to this (or any other) study group? What very practical steps can this group take to facilitate a deeper dialogue between and among its members?

5. Discuss whether you think that it is important to take your own stand in a community even if doing so provokes disagreement among members. What would happen if you withheld your stand? Would your relationship to the members of the group still be genuine?

6. What is your understanding of the connection between two key terms in this chapter—*meeting* and *relationship?* Describe a genuine connection that has occurred in your life. Did it lead to an ongoing relationship? If not, why? If so, describe the significance of that relationship in your life.

Notes

1. Although, for Buber, the "eternal *Thou*" happens through the "central *Thou*," the two *Thous* are not to be equated. Binding particular *I-Thou* relationships together, the "central *Thou*" is uniquely present in each community. The "eternal *Thou*," on the other hand, is everywhere eternally present.

2. Buber encountered Hasidism at an early age. At that time Hasidism represented for him an ideal religious community. However, the Hasidim in real life, which Buber did not understand at that time, excluded their wives from their religious way of life. A question remains, therefore, whether a community functioning under those circumstances can still be called a true community. Interestingly, Buber himself did not choose such a life.

3. Buber suggests that we cannot erase the boundaries between people and groups, but can only become "living answering for one another." In *Pointing The Way* he writes:

> The work of education unites the participating groups, through access to the educative forces and through common service to the facts, into a model of the great community. This community is no union of the like-minded, but a genuine living together of men of similar or of complementary natures but of differing minds. Community is the overcoming of *otherness* in living unity. (102)

Chapter 4

Who Is the "Real *I*"?

*The *I* is real in virtue of its sharing of reality. The fuller*
its sharing the more real it becomes.

This chapter is situated within two contexts, beginning with Buber's concern for the characteristics of genuine community discussed in Chapter 3. Authentic community, for Buber, arises from reciprocal relationships (1) with each person, and (2) with the "central *Thou*." While communal life cannot dispense with the world of experiencing and using, the very plasma of community is the spirit of relational trust permeating each *I-Thou* relationship in the group. The second context can be summarized by five brief remarks about the *I* who says "I." These are selected from the beginning of Part I, where Buber writes that

- there is no *I* by itself, but only the *I* of the *I-Thou* relationship, or the *I* of the *I-It* relation;

- when a person says "I," the speaker refers to one or the other of these primary relations;

- when a primary word is spoken, the speaker enters into the word and stands in it;

- whoever says "I perceive," "I feel," "I imagine," "I want," "I sense," "I think" remains in the realm of *I-It;* and

- whoever says *Thou* enters into genuine relationship.

Saying "I"

In *I and Thou* Buber uses the word *I* to designate either the person who enters into genuine interhuman relationship with another or someone who occupies a partial, one-sided relation with the other.

SMITH, 65 "TRUE SHIBBOLETH"	KAUFMANN, 115 "TRUE SHIBBOLETH"
The stronger the *I* of the primary word *I-Thou* is in the twofold *I,* the more personal is the man.	How much of a person a man is depends on how strong the I of the basic word I-You is in the human duality of his I.
According to his saying of *I*—according to what he means, when he says *I*—it can be decided where a man belongs and where his way leads. The word *I* is the true shibboleth of mankind.	The way he says I—what he means when he says I—decides where a man belongs and where he goes. The word "I" is the true shibboleth of humanity.
So listen to this word!	Listen to it!

But why, we might ask, does Buber insist here on the importance of listening to the way in which a person says "I"? According to Buber, the answer to that question is connected to the meaning of the Hebrew word *shibboleth.* For the ancient Hebrews, *shibboleth* literally meant a "test word" and was used to distinguish orthodox teaching and practice from unorthodox teaching and practice. The word has come to mean a "catchword" or a "motto" adopted by group members to identify their solidarity with one another.

Saying "I," therefore, connects me in solidarity to a species called human. But when we do say "I," according to Buber, we imply either the *I-Thou* mode of relationship or the *I-It* mode of relation to the world. In either mode I am responsible for the way that I say "I." Indeed, the way I say "I am," the way that I enter the "I," determines my bearing or stand in the world. This is especially true when I meet another person. In this sense *shibboleth* retains some of its old meaning.

Adam's Question

Throughout much of his life Buber was an ardent biblical reader, translator, and interpreter. He spent many years translating the Bible from Hebrew to German with his friend Franz Rosenzweig. One of the clearest examples of genuine dialogue in Buber's life was his relationship with Rosenzweig. Their friendship, which lasted till Rosenzweig's death in 1929, according to Rivka Horwitz (in *On the Way to Buber's "I and Thou"*), was one of rare reciprocity and was "characterized by a mutual give-and-take" (240). Their translation of the Bible, as we will note in Chapter 5, describes the provocative meeting between God and Moses, the famous "burning bush" story of Exodus, in language that captures both the original Hebrew and the philosophy of dialogue.

The meeting between God and Adam in the Book of Genesis, however, especially interested Buber, who began his little classic *The Way of Man: According to the Teachings of Hasidism* with a chapter titled "Heart-Searching." The chapter begins with a Hasidic story about the Genesis account of Adam's encounter with God: It is said that Rabbi Zalman was put in a Petersburg jail. While he was awaiting trial, the chief jailer entered his cell. However, since the rav was so deep in meditation, he did not at first notice his visitor. The chief jailer finally asked: "How are we to understand that God, the all-knowing, said to Adam: 'Where art thou?'"

In response, the rav said: "Do you believe that the Scriptures are eternal and that every era, every generation and every man is included in them?"

"I believe this," said the jailer.

"Well then" said the zaddik, "in every era, God calls to every person: 'where are you in your world?'"

After recording this story, Buber asks the reader to think again about what really happens in this tale, after the chief jailer asks about a passage from scripture. The rabbi tells his jailer, in effect: "You yourself are Adam, you are the man whom God asks: 'Where art thou?'" (9–12).

From the perspective of the philosophy of dialogue, the meaning of human life depends on how a person responds to this question. In *Between Man and Man* Buber writes that only when I enter relationship with my whole being am I really *there:*

> If to the call of present existence, "Where are you?" I answer, "Here I am!" but am not really there—that is to say, not there with the truth of my whole being—then I am guilty. (203)

Wholeness

Buber consistently refers to the question of personal presence by focusing on a philosophical version of God's question to Adam—namely, "What is man?" Buber's answer to this question can initially be discerned through his insistence on the wholeness of the human person. Wholeness, for him, refers to a seamless integration of body, mind, and spirit. In *Between Man and Man,* for example, the essential action of being human embodies "the wholeness of the person" (22). But not just wholeness—unique presence as well. For this reason Buber puts forward a remarkably innocent line: "The basic movement of the life of dialogue is the turning towards the other" (22). According to Buber, human wholeness includes

- our place in the cosmos;
- our connection with destiny;
- our relation to the world;
- our understanding of the other;
- our attitude towards the mystery of life's encounters; and
- our awareness of our own death.

Accordingly, a person's special place in creation involves a twofold perceptual dynamic: (1) "the primal setting at a distance," expressed in our awareness of the "other" as unique; and (2) entering into relationship. The act of distancing ourselves from the world is necessary in order to become an independent other, and this act makes room for relationship. Needless to say, relationship does not, however, necessarily follow from an act of distancing. These two movements characterize, according to Buber, "the whole person."

One can just as well set the other at a distance in order to enter an *I-It* form of dialogue. This kind of distancing does not constitute wholeness. But how is wholeness manifested? Is it really possible to become a "whole person"? It is not at all possible if one thinks that Buber means, by "whole," some action or set of actions—some way of life—that tries to conform to a definition of wholeness. Conforming to definitions and perceptions of wholeness does not make a person completely whole. Nor is personal wholeness a once-and-for-all state of being. Rather than a static precondition, realized wholeness is a direction of movement that comes and goes in particular, concrete moments.

Because wholeness is actualized in genuine moments of meeting, the phrase *whole person* indicates a direction of movement rather than the content of a belief. That is, wholeness embodies the presence of freedom in a healthy interplay between *I-Thou* and *I-It* modes of interaction. Illustrating this point, in the *Life of Dialogue* Maurice Friedman writes that an undivided person "responds with the whole...being to each new situation with no other preparation than...presence and...readiness to respond" (95). While directional movement and personal wholeness are prerequisites for genuine dialogue, both are made possible through dialogue itself. Personal wholeness always embodies a unique direction of movement along with a unique response to the concrete situation. Since genuine response is a response of the whole person, and since in every situation we respond in unique ways, one's wholeness in each situation is equally unique.

In this sense wholeness involves a direction of movement shaped by interactions between each person's unique presence.

Thus, one becomes more whole through a deeper expression of uniqueness in dialogue. In *Philosophical Interrogations* Buber summarizes what he means by wholeness in dialogue:

> "With the whole being" can be described most simply thus: I enter into the act or event which is in question with all the available forces of my soul without conflict, without even latent much less perceptible conflict. (52)

Recall that Buber's "wholeness" refers to a body-mind-spirit integration in which no one element is privileged. Incapable of subjection to quantitative measurement, genuine wholeness arises on both sides of real meeting between persons. It is there that "I am."

Unique Presence

Wholeness and unique presence, for Buber, are intimately and creatively connected. In *The Way of Man,* in a section entitled "The Particular Way," Buber reflects on a Hasidic story about the uniqueness of each person's life path. Buber writes: "Every person born into this world represents something new, something that never existed before, something original and unique" (16). In other words, every person is called to fulfill a particular direction of movement.

This same idea was expressed with even greater poignancy by Rabbi Zusya, who, a short while before dying, says: "In the world to come I shall not be asked: 'why were you not Moses?' I shall be asked: 'Why were you not Zusya?'" (17). Naturally, several questions of meaning arise from this Hasidic tale: Of what is my uniqueness composed? How do I become fully present in relationships? And is a dialogical person changed as a result of every human meeting?

Buber's response to questions like these uncovers multiple, creative tensions between some of our most cherished dualities: is and ought, hidden and revealed, personal and social. One enters most fully into relationship with another person through ongoing tensions between *choosing* to do so and *being chosen* to do so, and equally so in the tension between choosing to confirm the

101

other and choosing to contend *against* the other. Recall that, according to Buber, real humanness is not something that can be sought and found. It is not a product, not an idea that one tries to attain, but a personal direction discovered ever anew through concrete moments of meeting. If we aim at uniqueness or at wholeness, we wind up finding something else.

Accordingly, for Buber, I become uniquely present as I bring the ever-changing, never-having-before-been, and always-new dynamic embodied uniquely by each person into meetings with others. Figure 4–1 depicts ever-interacting tensions and directions of movement both encountered and embodied by dialogical persons.

Figure 4–1. Uniquely Present Person

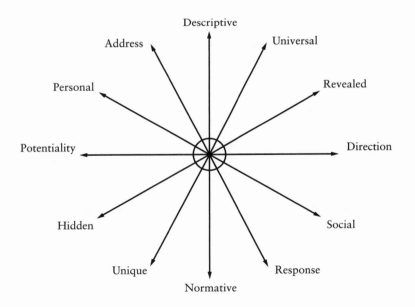

The action of stepping into direct relationship with others, wholeness to wholeness, involves the *surrender* of one's agenda, an intentional willingness to be chosen by another. The word *surrender* is not implied either by Smith's "suffering" or Kaufmann's "passivity,"

but it is a more appropriate translation for the German word *Passion* because it suggests letting go of self while still taking a uniquely personal stand. It means acting in seemingly opposing ways at the same time. To put it another way, for Buber, wholeness embodies suspending everything and anything that disallows me to be fully present in the moment (prejudices, assumptions, and so on), while still remaining uniquely myself without these. Speaking about the whole human person's place in genuine dialogue, Buber writes:

SMITH, 76–77
"WHOLE MAN"

KAUFMANN, 124–25
"WHOLE HUMAN BEING"

The *Thou* confronts me. But I step into direct relation with it. Hence the relation means being chosen and choosing, suffering and action in one; just as any action of the whole being which means the suspension of all partial actions, and consequently of all sensations of actions grounded only in their particular limitation, is bound to resemble suffering.

This is the activity of the man who has become a whole being, an activity that has been termed doing nothing: nothing separate or partial stirs in the man any more, thus he makes no intervention in the world; it is the whole man, enclosed and at rest in his wholeness, that is effective—he has become an effective whole. To have won stability in this state is to be able to go out to the supreme meeting.

The You confronts me. But I enter into a direct relationship to it. Thus the relationship is at once being chosen and choosing, passive and active. For an action of the whole being does away with all partial actions and thus also with all sensations of action (which depend entirely on the limited nature of actions)—and hence it comes to resemble passivity.

This is the activity of the human being who has become whole: it has been called not-doing, for nothing particular, nothing partial is at work in them and thus nothing in him intrudes into the world. It is the whole human being, closed in its wholeness, at rest in its wholeness, that is active here, as the human being has become an active whole. When one has achieved steadfastness in this state, one is able to venture forth to the supreme encounter.

Being really present, then, strangely enough involves "doing nothing" (Smith) or "not-doing" (Kaufmann). These translations, however, carry misleadingly negative connotations. Rather than "doing nothing" or "not-doing," Buber meant to suggest the presence—calm and self-contained—of non-doing, or doing-less doing. Here, Buber's ongoing interest in the teaching of the *Tao* and of *wu-wei* (action-less action) is evident. An activity of the completed or whole being entering into dialogue is a personal action that I undertake and, at the same time, that undertakes me.

The Interhuman

Another way to understand what Buber means by unique presence is to reconsider the interhuman realm, which occurs when meetings between persons are genuine. Buber readily admitted that the term *interhuman* cannot be identified either arithmetically or geometrically. The interhuman cannot be reduced to *"It,"* to a thing. Indeed, mental categories do not suffice to describe *I-Thou* dialogues because they reduce it to material substance, to an idea of the thing removed from the event itself. When speaking about the "interhuman," or "the between," Buber proceeds from the living, concrete situation of two persons engaged in genuine dialogue. Meaningful dialogue is not merely a physical phenomenon going on outside me or an internal psychic phenomenon but an indescribable unity that stands beyond the duality of the physical and psychic, or mental, realms.

More than the sum of personality traits, the interhuman is the *presence of spontaneous mutuality* that comes alive in and through powerful moments of genuine dialogue. In *Philosophical Interrogations* Buber writes: "I have only pointed out that we cannot do without [the between] for a full comprehension and presentation of what passes between two men when they stand in dialogue with each other" (27). If two persons—two separate, individual subjectivities—genuinely meet each other, a new reality is generated between them.

This third reality, "the interhuman," metaphorically located in "the between," is more than the sum of the dialogical partners. Buber uses several different images to describe its presence:

- the unfolding "between"

- interhuman wholeness

- immediate directness

- mutual presence

- vital reciprocity

- elemental togetherness

While it is possible to describe these elements, no matter how hard a person strives to enter "betweenness," no matter how deeply one intends it, "betweenness" thickens only through dynamic, interhuman graces that come and go. Relational grace arises from and generates real interactions between persons, and without real *bonding,* relational grace remains hidden.

Psychologizing the World

Perhaps we can better understand the meaning of Buber's relational language by placing his words against a backdrop of their opposite—the irrational, unreal, internalized "I." In his essay "On the Psychologizing of the World" (in *A Believing Humanism*) Buber speaks of the fundamentally difficult problem of human-kind's insistence on seeing the world through a psychological filter of judgments and assessments:

> Psychologizing of the world is the inclusion of the world in the soul, the transference of the world into the soul, but not just any such transference but only that which goes so far that the essential is thereby disturbed....This essential is the facing of I and world. That the world faces me and that between us the real happens, this essential basic relation from which our life receives its meaning is injured if the world is so far removed within the soul that its non-psychic reality is obliterated, that this fundamental relation of I to world ceases to be able to be a relation of I to Thou. (144)

The signs that some people are addicted to this internalizing process abound. Consider, for example, the many books, work-shops, and therapies aimed at the self. Think of spiritual move-ments such as the Self-Realization Fellowship of Paramahansa Yogananda or the following bookstore poster that invites one to awaken to true self.

> *Who Am I?*
> An
> Opportunity to
> Gently and deeply
> Explore yourself,
> Your views, and
> What lies
> Beyond.
> Retreat focused on
> Self-Knowledge
> Through clear
> Insight and
> Profound
> Understanding.

Terms such as *self-actualization,* and *self-realization,* and *realizing your potentialities* have become popular mantras recited by spiritual seekers. Internalizing everything in this way, however, though an indispensable stage, moves one away from potential wholeness and only reinforces the "I" side of human relations.

These psychologizing approaches to living do not address a more fundamental question: If I already am myself, what is it that I need to realize? If I am not the person I will become, then whatever I do to become that person won't add or subtract from who I am. Even worse, if I am fated to become what I will become, then I need not do anything to achieve it. For Buber, we do not control our own destinies or "actualize" ourselves. Instead, we become ourselves only when we meet others spontaneously. When left to itself without any contact with a *Thou,* the world of the individual becomes estranged. As long as I remain tucked away securely in my own self-consciousness, no matter how heightened, I continue to live outside of genuine relationship.

Person or Individual?

Part of the problem with psychologizing attitudes is that they overemphasize only one aspect of what we know as "selfhood." Buber describes the "I," which speaks the primary word *I-It,* as a self-willed individual *(Eigenwesen),* and it is this "I as individual" that the processes of psychology (professional or otherwise) reinforce. The "I" that becomes whole in the realm of *I-Thou* relationships Buber thinks of as the "I as a person." Smith's and Kaufmann's two translations of Buber's distinction give a sense of the difference between what we call an individual and what we know to be a person:

SMITH, 62 INDIVIDUALITY	KAUFMANN, 111–12 EGO
The *I* of the primary word *I-It* makes its appearance as individuality and becomes conscious of itself as subject (of experiencing and using).	The I of the basic word I-It appears as an ego and becomes conscious of itself as a subject (of experience and use).
The *I* of the primary word *I-Thou* makes its appearance as person and becomes conscious of itself as subjectivity (without a dependent genitive).	The I of the basic word I-You appears as a person and becomes conscious of itself as subjectivity (without any dependent genetive [sic]).
Individuality makes its appearance by being differentiated by other individualities.	Egos appear by setting themselves apart from other egos.
A person makes his appearance by entering into relation with other persons.	Persons appear by entering into relation with other persons.

A person lives *with* the world; the individual lives *in* the world. In a long footnote to his translation of *I and Thou*, Kaufmann indicates that *Eigenwesen* literally means "own-being," or "self-being." He quotes Buber's 1937 response to the first English translation of *I and Thou*, in which the word "individuality" was used. Buber wrote:

> In French there is the word *egotiste* (cf. Stendhal) which comes close to what I mean; but the English *Egotist* unfortunately means *Egoist,* and that is something else. Would it perhaps be possible to say: the egotical being? (112)[1]

The "I" that speaks the basic word *I-It* appears as a self-referencing, me-oriented individual and becomes conscious of itself as a subject who experiences and uses. This self-referencing individual makes its appearance and gives itself definition by setting itself up in isolation from other persons.

If the ego-oriented "individual" represents a partial aspect of one's existence, only really necessary for basic survival, the relationship-oriented "person" enlarges the unique human enterprise. It is important to notice that Buber's emphasis on the individual-person polarity signifies that both these tendencies are within each person. The distinction represents two poles of one's intrinsic humanity. No human being is either purely an "individual" or purely a "person." Each is twofold.

Becoming a Person

Admitting that his language necessarily creates intellectual idealizations, Buber speaks of the always-renewing process of becoming a "person." In Buber's terms, the "I" of the primal word *I-Thou* becomes a "person" by responsibly entering into genuine relationships.

Recall here the often-quoted aphorism from Part I of *I and Thou*: "I become through my relation to the *Thou*; as I become *I*, I say *Thou*" (Smith, 11). Buber suggests that one is not a "person" until he or she becomes a "person" with other persons. That is, you are not authentically human until you engage other humans by venturing forth into relationships while at the same time continuing to live your stand.

If an *individual,* by definition, remains separate from other individuals, then a *person* is one who enters in relationship with others. The former breaks away; the latter seeks interrelatedness. The *Thou*-itself-as-*I* lives not through experiencing and using but through *I-Thou* meetings. We can say that a person turns toward relationship and an individual turns toward individuality. The self-referencing individual is concerned with his or her "me-ness"—his kind, her race, his accomplishments, her genius:

INDIVIDUAL	PERSON
Ego-oriented; separated from others	Relationship-oriented; with others
Breaks away from relational events	Seeks interrelation
Experiences and uses	Realizes contact with others
Characterized by self-consciousness	Characterized by turning toward
Being so and none other	Becoming dialogical
Seeming	Unfolding

The Real *I*

Having spoken about "the personal present" that is represented through "the purely evocative word," Buber summarizes his emphasis on the interrelational person this way:

SMITH, 63 "THE *I* IS REAL"	KAUFMANN, 113 "THE I IS ACTUAL"
He who takes his stand in relation shares in reality, that is, in a being that neither	Whoever stands in relation, participates in an actuality; that is, in a being that is

merely belongs to him nor merely lies outside him. All reality is an activity in which I share without being able to appropriate for myself. Where there is no sharing there is no reality. Where there is self-appropriation there is no reality. The more direct the contact with the *Thou,* the fuller is the sharing.

The *I* is real in virtue of its sharing in reality. The fuller its sharing the more real it becomes.

neither merely a part of him nor merely outside him. All actuality is an activity in which I participate without being able to appropriate it. Where there is no participation, there is no actuality. Where there is self-appropriation, there is no actuality. The more directly the You is touched, the more perfect is the participation.

The I is actual through its participation in actuality. The more perfect the participation is, the more actual the I becomes.

To help clarify Buber's meaning, consider how Pamela Vermes (in *Buber on God and the Perfect Man*) begins a chapter entitled "The Real and Unified I":

The second stage of Buber's way is that, from having cultivated the habit of relation, the *I* becomes more real and more unified. These conditions are inseparable from one another, since a real *I* must be unified, and a unified *I* must be real, but they are not identical. (208)

The "I" becomes real through genuine participation in dialogue, but learning simply how to "unify the I" doesn't solve the problem. Attaining authenticity, each person in a unique way, occurs when the person is called forth to respond authentically in the world. Moreover, though no one alone is no more purely real or unreal than anyone else, *"I"* becomes more and more real through meetings with unique others. The "unified " is a personal direction of movement in which one chooses interhuman reality over individual realities.

What then unites the "real *I*" and the "unified *I,*" from a Hasidic point of view, is embodied in the "Counsels of Perfection" or "Wholeness." According to the Baal-Shem-Tov, the legendary founder of Hasidism, holiness is within the reach of all humans:

"REAL *I*" IN RELATION TO GOD	"UNIFIED *I*" IN RELATION TO ONESELF
1. Cleaving	1. Self-reflection
2. Humility	2. Unique Task
3. Holy Intention	3. Determination
4. Worship	4. Beginning with Yourself
5. Ardor	5. Not Being Preoccupied with Yourself
6. Joy	6. Standing Here

The similarities between these two lists are striking and suggestive. The "real *I*" sequence involves a person's relationship of cleaving, humility, and holy intention to God through worship, ardor, and joy. "Humility" arises from abandoning self-preoccupation. "Holy intention" is initiated by "beginning with oneself." "Worship" involves "determination." "Ardor" is a "unique task." And "joy" results spontaneously from "self-reflection."

Both lists characterize what Buber called (in *Hasidism and Modern Man*) "the fully realized whole person *[der vollkommenen Mensch]*" (51). Becoming a "unified I" involves relationship, self-reflection, and determination to and for oneself. The conundrum is this: While practicing the dedicated and unifying task of self-cultivation for the sake of genuine dialogue, the Hasidic tradition implores us not to take our "selves" too seriously.

Buber's ongoing interest in Taoism is once again evident. In a 1910 essay, "The Teaching of the Tao" (in *Pointing the Way*), Buber points out that the whole meaning of the Tao is "this unity which is grasped as the absolute" (46) in the genuine life.[2] For the way of the Tao, according to Buber, points to an image of the human: "the path of the perfected man" (35–38). And the perfected person does not seek to self-reify.

Dialogical Person

What Buber means by the "real *I*" is nothing more, and nothing less, than a "dialogical person." The dialogical person spontaneously, freely, directly, and mutually enters into *I-Thou* relationships.[3] Along with the analogous distinction between the individual and the person, Buber also makes a distinction between the "un-free man" and the "free man." The free person, believing in the real solidarity of *I* and *Thou* relationships, is continually open to "signs of address" that come from this present moment, in which he or she becomes aware that *he or she* is the person addressed.

SMITH, 59–60 FREE MAN/ SELF-WILLED MAN	KAUFMANN, 108–9 FREE MAN/ CAPRICIOUS MAN
The free man is he who wills without arbitrary self-will. He believes in reality, that is, he believes in the real solidarity of the real twofold entity *I* and *Thou*....He knows that he must go out with his whole being. The matter will not turn out according to his decision; but what is to come will come only when he decides on what he is able to will....	Free is the man who wills without caprice. He believes in the actual, which is to say: he believes in the real association of the real duality, I and You....He must go forth with his whole being: that he knows. It will not turn out the way his resolve intended it; but what wants to come will come only if he resolves to do that which he can will....
The self-willed man does not believe and does not meet. He does not know solidarity of connexion, but only the feverish world of outside and his feverish desire to use it.	The capricious man does not believe and encounter. He does not know association; he only knows the feverish world out there and his feverish desire to use it.

This passage is based on the necessary interplay between two types of persons who communicate in the world:

UN-FREE PERSON	REAL PERSON
Conditional Individuality	Unique Wholeness
Arbitrary Self-Will, or Willfulness	True Relational Will
Uses Others for His or Her Own Purposes	Experiences the Other's Side
Decisions Made Within the Person	Decisions Made Within the Dialogue
Self-reflection: Bending Back on Oneself	Turning One's Whole Person Toward Dialogue

Genuine and Demonic Dialogue

Buber offers three historical examples of what he calls the "free man" of "genuine dialogue": Goethe, who related genuinely to nature; Socrates, who entered deeply into dialogue with humans; and Jesus, who dedicated himself to the "eternal *Thou.*" For Buber, with Goethe, with Socrates, and with Jesus, the saying of "I" embodies the purely "personal," with scarcely a trace of "individuality" *(Eigenwesen)*. In these three, Buber argues, we find representatives of persons in genuine dialogue who became liberated from the constrains of self-concern in much of their work.

SMITH, 66–67 "ENDLESS DIALOGUE"	KAUFMANN, 115–16 "INFINITE CONVERSATION"
But how lovely and how fitting the sound of the lively and the impressive *I* of Socrates! It is the *I* of endless dialogue and the air of dialogue is wafted around it in all its journeys, before the judges, and in the last hour in prison. This *I* lived continually in the relation with man which is bodied forth in dialogue....	But how beautiful and legitimate the vivid and empathic I of Socrates sounds! It is the I of infinite conversation, and the air of conversation is present in all its ways, even before his judges, even in the final hour in prison. This I lived in that relation to man which is embodied in conversation....

How lovely and how legitimate the soul of the full *I* of Goethe! It is the *I* of pure intercourse with nature; nature gives herself to it and speaks unceasingly with it, revealing her mysteries to it but not betraying her mystery....

And to anticipate by taking an illustration from the realm of unconditional relation: how powerful, even to being overpowering, and how legitimate, even to being self-evident, is the saying of *I* by Jesus! For it is the *I* of unconditional relation in which the man calls his *Thou* Father in such a way that he himself is simply Son, and nothing else but Son. Whenever he says *I* he can only mean the *I* of the wholly primary word that has been raised for him into unconditional being.

How beautiful and legitimate the full I of Goethe sounds! It is the I of pure intercourse with nature. Nature yields to it and speaks unceasingly with it; she reveals her mysteries to it and yet does not betray her mystery....

And to anticipate and choose an image from the realm of unconditional relation: how powerful, even overpowering, is Jesus' I-saying, and how legitimate to the point of being a matter of course! For it is the I of the unconditional relation in which man calls his You "Father" in such a way that he himself becomes nothing but a son. Whenever he says I, he can only mean the I of the wholly basic word that has become unconditional for him.

All three figures embody "spirit taking form." Goethe created form through art, Socrates through formal ideas, and Jesus through expressions of wisdom. Each of their manifestations of "spirit" points to what awaits, just parallel to common life.[4]

As an anti-hero, or a disingenuous "I," Buber offers the figure of Napoleon, who was not a genuine "I" but a demonic expression of the life of monologue. Napoleon spoke "I" not relationally but impersonally, as the executer of fateful decrees. Like Hitler, Napoleon recognized only his association with a cause. For him, no one can become a *Thou*. The possibility of mutuality disappears. Napoleon went so far as to treat himself as an *It*. He became an impersonal "I," executing the decrees even against his own self-reified self, married to an ideology. Hitler became a kind of incarnation of Napoleon for Buber: a pseudo-*Thou.*

Like Napoleon, Hitler became possessed by himself. In this way Napoleon and Hitler (and others like them) bring one up against the limits of dialogue, when the other refuses to respond genuinely, or at all. In *The Philosophy of Martin Buber* Buber refers to what he calls "dialogical powerlessness" to describe the relationship between Hitler and the rest of the world:

> Hitler is not my antagonist in the sense of a partner "whom I can confirm in opposing him,"...for he is incapable of really addressing one and incapable of really listening to one. That I once experienced personally when, if only through the technical medium of the radio, I heard him speak. I knew that this voice was in the position to annihilate me together with countless of my brothers and sisters; but I perceived that despite such might [his voice] was not in the position to set the spoken and heard word into the world. (725–26)

An implicit terror lurks behind this remark. What does a person do when "the great dialogue between I and Thou is silent," when "nothing else exists than his self"? (x). At this point we come to understand more deeply why Buber continually insisted upon the need to enter genuine dialogues with others. "Only so," he said upon receiving the Peace Prize of the German Book Trade in 1953, "can conflict certainly not be eliminated from the world but be humanly arbitrated and led to its overcoming" (*Pointing the Way,* 238).

Jesus

Buber addresses the figure of Jesus in *Two Types of Faith,* having noted elsewhere that Jews know Jesus from within, in the impulses and stirrings of his being: "From my youth onwards I found in Jesus my great brother." And he adds: "My own fraternally open relationship to him has grown even stronger and clearer, and to-day I see him more strongly and clearly than ever before" (12). Buber's image of Jesus is of a fully unique, fully human person who related to God unconditionally as a son. Maurice Friedman indicates that, for Buber, Jesus stands on the human side of the dialogue with God. In *Encounter on the Narrow Ridge* Friedman writes:

> Buber did not see Jesus' uniqueness as consisting of something in him—a power in itself—for this would mean to empty the real, the present relation, of reality. Rather, Jesus's uniqueness lay in the strength, the immediacy, the unconditionality of the "between." (140)

According to Buber, when Jesus spoke of the unconditional love, he referred to the immediate realm of unconditional dialogue. God's kingdom is a here-and-now kingdom that occurs among persons in genuine relationships. This understanding reflects the Hasidic way of being "humanly holy." As a "servant of YHWH," Jesus spoke the unfathomable depths of God's wisdom in simple stories and parables. The relation, for Buber, between Jesus' parables and Hasidic tales, or legendary anecdotes, is both clearly evident and significant. Consider the suggestive connections between them: Each is part of the oral tradition; each embodies deep wisdom; each invites listeners into a dialogue with the parable or tale; and each embodies a double message: turn *(teshuvah)* and trust *(emunah)*.[5]

But who was the historical Jesus of Nazareth? What manner of person was he? Biblical commentators suggest that Jesus (his Jewish name was Yeshua) was an itinerant teacher who often spoke with authority in parables. According to Buber, Jesus' teaching stories are formed from the preserved nucleus of authentic conversations that once took place between Jesus and the disciples. Along with acts of blessing, empowering compassion, mercy, healing, and caution, Jesus entered into genuine dialogues with his disciples at meals, while walking between villages, and after prayer. At the heart of these genuine interactions, Jesus' words were spoken as command, question, and encouragement.

Unwaveringly, according to Buber, Jesus' central message announces that the kingdom of God is already breaking into the present situation and that those who really hear the message are called upon to turn and trust. Although the ethical and eschato-logical *content* of Jesus' teaching varied according to the setting, its *form* did not. When Jesus' parables are surveyed, one sees how significant this distinction between content and form is. But why? Because, for one reason, Jesus never explains to the listener what his parables mean. Rather, within a familiar context Jesus challenges ordinary thinking and usual behavior, and opens new possibilities for living. The listener then is invited to continue his or her interaction with Jesus as a living parable.

In Buber's view, therefore, Jesus taught and was always willing to enter into unconditional dialogues with others and with God. He invited his disciples to do the same. Yet, despite the immediate and this-worldly form of Jesus' teachings, theologians have often privileged the ethical and eschatological content of his message. But what is essential about Jesus, according to Buber, is the situation-specific meetings between himself and his friends and enemies, which are embodied in his parables and his life.

One sees the significance of *I-Thou* dialogue for Jesus, for example, in his saying "Where two or three are gathered in my name, there I am in their midst" (Matt 18:20). Applying Buber's dialogic principles to this saying of Jesus, the term "gathered" suddenly takes on a new significance. It suggests not just a collective social or economic purpose but a genuine togetherness, a community of conversations by which persons really meet one another. The spirit of Jesus is thereby recognized in our "midst."[6]

Trembling at Alienation

Buber concludes Part II of *I and Thou* by reflecting lyrically about the possible dangers of the world of *It*. There are times, he writes, when a person shudders "at the alienation between the I and the world" and "comes to reflect that something is to be done" (Smith, 70). But when one realizes that the I has become submerged in the world of *It*, or that the world has become stuffed into the bag of perceptions called the personal ego, what is to be done? At this point, Buber does something quite unusual for him:

He introduces a specific practice to untangle the nightmare mesh of self-withdrawal:

SMITH, 70
TURNING

As when in the grave night-hour you lie, racked by waking dream—bulwarks have fallen away and the abyss is screaming—and note amid your torment: there is still life, if only I got through to it—but how, how?; so is this man in the hours of reflection, shuddering, and aimlessly considering this and that. And perhaps away in the unloved knowledge of the depths within him, he really knows the direction of turning, leading through sacrifice.

KAUFMANN, 120
RETURN

Imagine that at some dreadful midnight you lie there, tormented by a waking dream: the bulwarks have crumbled and the abysses scream, and you realize in the midst of this agony that life is still there and I must merely get through to it—but how? how? Thus feels man in the hours when he collects himself: overcome by horror, pondering, without direction. And yet he may know the right direction, deep down in the unloved knowledge of the depths—the direction of return that leads through sacrifice.

Here we arrive at Buber's first significant reference to one of his most central addresses—the act of "turning." Turning, as we shall see, comes through surrendering self-will and willfulness, leading away from separateness and individuality toward relationship with the other. "Turning" is one of the six leading addresses of *I and Thou* and will be taken up in greater detail in Chapter 6.

Meetings

To help take us deeper into the meaning of Buber's address in this chapter, we include here a well-known anecdote that

Buber tells about himself in an earlier book, *Daniel: Dialogues on Realization* (1913). The anecdote ponders the significance of discovering a piece of mica.

Mica

And now I shall tell you Lukas, how the final level of the teaching ripened in me and how the teaching arose. But there is almost nothing more to tell. I said it to you already, in fact: a moment joined itself to a moment. On a gloomy morning I walked upon the highway, saw a piece of mica lying, lifted it up and looked at it for a long time; the day was no longer gloomy, so much light was caught in the stone. And suddenly as I raised my eyes from it, I realized that while I looked I had not been conscious of "object" and "subject"; in my looking the mica and "I" had been one; in my looking I had tasted unity. I looked at it again, the unity did not return. But there it burned in me as though to create. I closed my eyes, I gathered my strength, I bound myself with my object, I raised the mica into the kingdom of the existing. And there, Lukas, I first felt: *I, there I first was I.* The one who looked had not yet been I; only this man here, this unified man, bore the name like a crown. Now I perceived that first unity as the marble statue may perceive the block out of which it was chiseled; it was the undifferentiated, I was the unification. Still I did not understand myself; but then there flashed through me the memory: thus had my body fifteen human years before done the simple deed and, the fingers entwined, united life and death to "I." (140–41)

In this extraordinary experience, while looking at a piece of mica, the young Buber suddenly "tasted unity" by realizing that he was momentarily not conscious of subject or object. Then, years later, in hindsight, Buber could say that "I was the unification."

A few years later, in *I and Thou,* Buber would recall this event:

SMITH, 98 "FRAGMENT OF MICA"	KAUFMANN, 146–47 "FRAGMENT OF MICA"
How powerful is the unbroken world of *It,* and how delicate are the appearances of the *Thou!*	How powerful is the continuum of the It-world, and how tender the manifestation of the You!
So much can never break through the crust of the condition of things! O fragment of mica, looking on which I once learned, for the first time, that *I* is not something "in me"—with you I was nevertheless only bound up in myself; at that time the event took place only in me, not between me and you. But when one that is alive rises out of things, and becomes a being in relation to me, joined to me by its nearness and its speech, for how inevitable short a time is it nothing to me but *Thou!* It is not the relation that necessarily grows feeble, but the actuality of its immediacy.	There is so much that can never break through the crust of thinghood! O fragment of mica, it was while contemplating you that I first understood that I is not something "in me"—yet I was associated with you only in myself; it was only in me, no between you and me that it happened that time. But when something does emerge from among things, something living, and becomes a being for me, and comes to me, near and eloquent, how unavoidably briefly it is for me nothing but You! It is not the relationship that necessarily wanes, but the actuality of its directness.

While looking at the fragment of mica, Buber makes the powerful discovery that the *"I"* is not something *"in me."* Rather, the "real *I,*" my true self, emerges in "genuine dialogue," in presentness, freedom, direction, and mutuality. This dialogic realization clearly sets Buber apart from other philosophers for whom the "I" is known primarily *within* the self. Of course, the idea that we become ourselves most genuinely with others does imply that we owe our ability to become human to our partners. Rather, becoming human is owed to *relationship* itself. Our foremost task, therefore, is to fulfill our unique, unpredictable, ever-recurring potentialities by hallowing the everyday with others.

Practice Exercises

1. How do I become *"I"*? Give examples.

2. What is the major personal insight in this chapter for you? Describe it, first in Buber's words, then in your own. Offer an example of how to apply this insight. Discuss your example in dialogue with others.

3. Does "the between" have a location? If so, where does it exist? What is it that generates "the between?" And why is "the between" so crucial for Buber? Recall an event in your life in which "the between" became almost palpable.

4. Consider this statement: I have to know myself first before I can really know anyone else. How would Buber respond to this statement? How do you respond to it? Can one come to know one's self before knowing another?

5. Compare the two versions of the mica story. What does Buber add to the original mica story when he retells it in *I and Thou?* What difference does this make?

6. Do you agree with Buber that *"I* is not something 'in me'"? When you say "I," how do you take your stand in the world? What expectations do you have? How do you view the other?

Notes

1. Following Buber, for our purposes it is necessary to qualify both Smith's "individual" and Kaufmann's "ego" at this point. On the one hand, the "I" of the basic word *I-It* appears as a self-referencing, ego-oriented individual and becomes conscious of itself as a subject who

experiences and uses. On the other hand, this self-referencing individual sets itself up in isolation from other persons.

2. In his comparative study *I and Tao,* Jonathan Herman suggests the possibility that *I and Thou* was significantly influenced by the Taoist philosopher Chuang Tzu. Rejecting the standard view that Buber's initial engagement with Taoism marks a transitional philosophical stage, Herman contends "that the fundamental ingredients of I-Thou relationship are in fact already present within Buber's encounter with *Chuang Tzu*" (163). Following this interpretive view, one can say that Buber's *I and Thou* describes the way of dialogue.

3. In "A Dialogical View of the Person" (in *Contemporary Psychology*), Maurice Friedman writes: "In the dialogical view we become persons in what Martin Buber calls the 'I-Thou' relationship—the direct, reciprocal, present relation between the person and what comes to meet him or her as opposed to the indirect, non-mutual, relation of 'I-It.' I-Thou is a dialogue in which the other is accepted in his or her unique otherness and not reduced to a content of my experience" (23).

4. When Buber talks about Goethe, both translations are inaccurate. They should read: "Nature yields to *him* and speaks unceasingly with *him*, revealing her mysteries to *him*, but yet does not give away her mystery." Buber speaks here about Goethe's relationship to nature, and nature's response to Goethe. These glowing descriptions do not mean to suggest that Buber had no disagreements with these figures. With regard to Socrates in *Philosophical Interrogations*, Buber writes:

> I know of very few men in history to whom I stand in such a relation of both trust and veneration as Socrates. But when it is a matter of using "Socratic questions" as an educational method I am against it. [He then added] Socrates conducts his dialogue by posing questions and proving the answers that he received untenable; these are no real questions; they are moves in a sublime dialectical game that has a goal, the goal of revealing a not-knowing. But when the teacher…enters into a dialogue with his pupil and in this connection directs a question to him, he asks, as the simple man who is not inclined to dialectic asks because he wants to know something. (67)

This quotation demonstrates both Buber's admiration for Socrates as well as a fundamental difference between them. It is especially instructive to note Buber's response to Socrates' method of dialogue. According to Buber, genuine dialogue does not embody trying to obtain a prior goal but remains open to the possibility of a change of viewpoints occurring on each side.

5. In *Two Types of Faith* Buber applies his understanding of *teshuvah* to Jesus. In the earliest gospel, Mark, Jesus' first words are reported as these: "The time has come and the kingdom of God is at hand. Repent *[metanoia],* and believe in the Good News" (Mark 1:15). From the point of view that Jesus *(Yeshua)* spoke Hebrew and Aramaic, Buber writes that the earliest preaching of Jesus runs: "The appointed time is fulfilled and God's rule has come near. *Turn* and believe in the message" (italics added). Further, Buber indicates that Jesus' first message was likely: "*Turn* and *trust*" (125). And in *On Judaism* Buber grounds the first teaching of Jesus in the traditional teaching of *teshuvah.* Buber writes:

> The motive power of Jesus' message is the ancient Jewish demand for the unconditioned decision, a decision that transforms a man and lifts him into the divine realm. (70)

6. In a "Report on Two Talks" (quoted here from *Eclipse of God*), Buber writes: "For where two or three are truly together, they are together in the name of God" (9). If one juxtaposes Buber's line with Jesus' statement, it can be said that being gathered in Jesus' name suggests being "truly together" in the presence of mutuality with others. Gatherings of two or three, at the time of Jesus, would have been for prayer, study, or decision-making. In that context this verse can be said to evoke the "sonship of Jesus" as the "spirit" of trusting togetherness emerging from the midst of persons in genuine dialogue.

The "I" of Jesus, according to Buber in *I and Thou,* is the "I" of the solidarity of unconditional relationship, the "I" of "the holy primary word that has been raised for him into unconditional being" (Smith, 67). Jesus speaks to others only out of the abiding solidarity of *I* and *Thou.* On the last page of *I and Thou,* for example, in a way echoing Jesus' words, Buber writes that the kingdom of authentic relationship, of genuine dialogue, "is hidden in our midst" (Smith, 120).

123

PART III

HALLOWING THE EVERYDAY

This is the eternal revelation which is present in the here and now. I neither know of nor believe in any revelation that is not the same in its primal phenomenon.

—MARTIN BUBER (Kaufmann, 160)

Chapter 5

Glimpsing the "Eternal *Thou*"

Every particular *Thou* is a glimpse through to the eternal
Thou; by means of every particular *Thou* the primary word
addresses the eternal *Thou.*

In Part I we described Buber's Generating Grid. We discussed the reciprocal movement between the *I-Thou* and *I-It* word pairs and four interlacing realms of relationship—with nature, with spirit becoming forms, with persons, and with the "eternal *Thou.*" In Part II we shifted our consideration to two reciprocal interhuman out-flowings of genuine *I-Thou* relationship: the dynamic immediacy central to genuine community, and the innermost reality of the true person. Discussing this sense of community in Chapter 3, we focused on Buber's description of genuine community as a vital intersection between persons standing toward a "living center" and toward each other in reciprocal giving and receiving. And in Chapter 4 we pondered three interrelated prerequisites for becoming *human:* (1) personal wholeness; (2) unique presence; and (3) responding to every concrete situation without imposing one's own direction onto it.

The third and last part of *I and Thou* (spanning Chapters 5 and 6) is largely devoted to the relationship between "I" and the "eternal *Thou*," and with the dialogically oriented movement Buber calls "turning." Buber's image of God has been briefly mentioned through Parts I and II as the "eternal *Thou*," who can be glimpsed in every genuine *I-Thou* relationship. To underscore the transcendent implications of Buber's thought, it is important to recall that for Buber every genuine dialogue can become transparent to the presence of the "eternal *Thou*."

We begin this chapter, then, with two statements Buber made toward the end of his life that reinforce his "most essential concern"—the interaction between God and humans. In *Philosophical Interrogations* he writes:

> If I myself should designate something as the "central portion of my life work," then it could not be anything individual, but only the one basic insight that has led me not only to the study of the Bible, as to the study of Hasidism, but also to an independent philosophical presentation: that the I-Thou relation to God and the I-Thou relation to one's fellow man are at bottom related to each other. (99)

And in *The Philosophy of Martin Buber* he notes that he was and remained "simply concerned that both [human and supernatural] relationships are essentially similar, because both signify the direct turning to a Thou and both find their fulfillment in actual reciprocity" (694). Given the profound significance of the divine-human relationship, we should consider what Buber has to say about it, and what parallels exist between *I-Thou* and *I*-God relationships.

Knowing God

A headline in the February 25, 2001, edition of the Santa Cruz *Sentinel* reads: "Deepak Chopra talks about how to know God." The reporter begins by indicating that listening to Deepak Chopra speak about God is a "soul-satisfying" experience. In his book *How to Know God*, the article continues, Chopra writes that the answer to this question about how to know God does not lie with God. Rather, it lies with our interpretation of God.

Chopra's book attempts to correct what he considers a common misconception, that is, that God can only be known through the mind and the brain. According to Chopra, there are in fact seven ways in which we can come to know God. We can know God as

- God the Protector,

- God the Almighty,

- The God of Peace,

- God the Redeemer,

- God the Creator,

- The God of Miracles, and

- The God of Pure Being—the "I am."

With regard to the seventh way of knowing God, Chopra adds that the observer, the person in dialogue with God, collapses and integrates into the thing observed. When he or she reaches this level of God-realization, all separation ends.

Buber does not, nor would he, speak this way. While Buber writes that God is not an interpretation of God, he takes this assertion in a different direction. Since God cannot be known through the mind, when we list seven aspects of God, we are simply articulating another mental interpretation. Of course, the idea that we collapse into oneness with God at the highest level of relationship can only be classified as another concept of who God is.

In place of offering an interpretation of who God is, Buber posits that the *presence* of God is glimpsed through the interhuman realm. According to Buber, we glimpse God not with our "mind's eye" but with our "being's eye." Reinforcing this point, Buber writes in *Eclipse of God* that "this glance of the being exists, wholly unillusory, yielding no images yet first making possible all images" (127). That is, God cannot be spoken of in the third person, is not an idea, is not even a mystical experience.

Buber would likely have questioned the way that the question of how we know God is put forward. In May of 1914, before the outbreak of World War I, Buber was asked a very similar question by a friend: "Do you believe in God?" Buber had a difficult time making a genuine reply because he did not reflect on God in that way, as a thing known and believed in. Only later, as he reflected on this, did he come to formulate a response that he recounted in *Meetings*:

> "If to believe in God means to be able to talk about him in the third person, then I do not believe in God. If to believe in him means to be able to talk to him, then I believe in God." And after a while, further: "The God...to whom Daniel prays in his suffering is my God and the God of all." (44)

Adam's Challenge

Entering dialogue, whether with humans or with God, for Buber, begins when we recognize, figuratively speaking, that we are, like Adam, called to answer the question Where are you? whenever it is personally addressed to us. By asking it, the "eternal *Thou*" evokes a response from Adam's side of dialogue. By answering it, we realize our uniquely human task of entering into genuine dialogue with the one who is present with us.

Buber's philosophical response to this question of God was shaped by his reflecting on the puzzling differences between what God *says* and what God actually *does* in the Book of Genesis:

> Then God said, "Let us make man in our image, after our likeness, to have dominion over the fish in the sea, the birds of the air, the cattle, all wild animals on land, and everything that creeps on the earth." (Gen 1:26)

In this first verse God is going to create humans in God's own likeness. But God ultimately, in the very next verse, creates humans only in the *image* of God: "In the image of God He created them. Male and female He created them" (Gen 1:27). Had God abandoned the first divine covenant? This discrepancy challenged Buber to the core.

When Buber considered what the ancient Rabbis said about the discrepancy between these two verses, it became more and more apparent to him that he was being addressed by this question personally. Buber found one provocative answer to the conundrum in a rabbinic interpretation: "Likeness lies in the hand of man." What Adam had failed to do, Buber now felt called to rectify. That is, Buber felt called to carry forth Adam's task. He only had to discover what that task was. In Buber's mind, Adam mistook God's original intention in creation. Adam didn't realize that he had to work toward perfecting the image of God placed inside him. Buber came to recognize in these verses his life purpose. And not just his alone. He understood this to be the task of all people who recognize God's address to them. The task is to become a partner *with* God in creation.

But how?

First, we must cut away our mind-forged perceptions of God, what Buber calls in *Philosophical Interrogations* our "passionate devotion to a fantasy image that one regards as God" (81). In a book of essays, *Israel and the World,* Buber writes that we enter a creative partnership with God by "imitating God," by "cleaving to God's ways," and not by constructing God from our imaginations. Instructively, he writes that one walks in the footsteps of the divine presence by imitating God's "attributes." The attributes, of course, are not imagined or thought up but expressed, literally spoken from God's position in our dialogue with the "eternal *Thou.*"

The modes (or attributes) in which God works, so far as they can be known, appear in the Torah in various forms and were referred to by Buber as follows:

- God *clothed* the nakedness of the first human beings;

- God *visited* Abraham when he was sick;

- God *comforted* Isaac with a blessing after Abraham's death; and

- God *buried* Moses. (76, italics added)

It is important, according to Buber, to learn to imitate God's handicraft by serving one another, by visiting and comforting one another, even by standing with one another in the presence of death.

Toward the end of the third Part of *I and Thou* Buber writes: "Even though we earthly beings never look at God without the world but only look at the world in God, yet as we look we form eternally God's countenance" (Smith, 119). The countenance of God *(Gottes Gestalt)* becomes present again and again through the unique particularities of everyday relationships. Buber writes, therefore, that God is always close to humans as long as humans do not distance themselves from one another. This, he concludes, is Adam's task: to preserve and confirm the image of God in his fellow human beings.

The "Eternal *Thou*"

Buber begins Part III by drawing together what we might consider the culminating or ultimate situation of *I-Thou* relationships. The extended lines of genuine relationships allow us to glimpse the presence of the "eternal *Thou*."

SMITH, 75 ETERNAL *THOU*	KAUFMANN, 123 ETERNAL YOU
Every particular *Thou* is a glimpse through to the eternal *Thou;* by means of every particular *Thou* the primary word addresses the eternal *Thou*. Through this mediation of the *Thou* of all beings fulfilment, and non-fulfilment, of relations comes to them: the inborn *Thou* is realized in each relation and consummated in none. It is consummated only in the direct relation with the *Thou* that by its nature cannot become *It*.	Every single You is a glimpse of that. Through every single You the basic word addresses the eternal You. The mediatorship of the You of all beings accounts for the fullness of our relationships to them—and for the lack of fulfillment. The innate You is actualized each time without ever being perfected. It attains perfection solely in the immediate relationship to the You that in accordance with its nature cannot become an It.

What Buber says here is of such significance that it would be helpful for us to re-consider it in a simpler form:

- The extended directions of genuine relationships meet in God;

- Every particular genuine relationship is a window to the "eternal *Thou*";

- The "inborn *Thou*" is realized in each genuine relationship without being consummated; and

- The "inborn *Thou*" is only consummated in relationship with the "eternal *Thou*."

Even though God cannot be "expressed" as an idea, the presence of God can be "addressed." One comes "before the face" of God through genuine meetings with a "particular *Thou*." Our relationships with each other are never complete in and of themselves. In fact, the act of relationship is never fully consummated at all except in the presence of the "eternal *Thou*." God, therefore, is the source and presence reflected by authentic relationship. As Buber would later write, "True address from God directs [us] into the place of lived speech, where the voices of the creatures grope past one another, and in their very missing of one another succeed in reaching the eternal partner" (*Between Man and Man*, 15).

While a continuous succession of *Thou*-moments is impossible to achieve, nevertheless a hidden *Thou*-world, based upon all relationships between *I* and *Thou,* runs alongside all human activity. This statement is pregnant with meaning, because, by its very nature, the "eternal *Thou*" cannot become an *I* and therefore must remain consistently immanent. This perception suggests at least two things: (1) that God can never become a particular being among many, or the sum total of all, because as "eternal *Thou*" God is the *Thou* of all *Thous;* and (2) that whatever else God is, God's full and meaningful *presen*ce is reflected in the presentness *(Gegenwart)* of genuine interactions.

Moreover, the "absolute *Thou*" forms a living bond among all separated beings. Every real relationship into which a person enters further clarifies the *I-Thou* relationship. Because it steps forth out of relationship, the true continuity of the "eternal *Thou*" cannot be deduced but can only be glimpsed. Each genuinely mutual relationship opens a curtain that separates us from the deepest space in which it is possible to glimpse the eternal address that calls out to us as "*Thou*."

Figure 5–1. Glimpsing the Eternal Thou

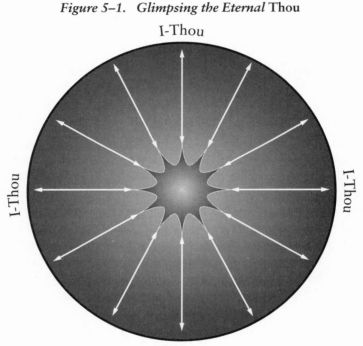

Mysterium Tremendum

According to Buber, God is altogether "Other," yet also altogether "Same" and altogether "Present."[1] Following Rudolf Otto's emphasis on religious immediacy in his 1917 book *The Idea of The Holy*, Buber's *I-Thou* God is the *Mysterium Tremendum* (the Tremendous Mystery). But God is also "nearer to me than my *I*," closer to me than myself. *Mysterium*, for Buber, meant that which is concealed beyond apprehension or conceptual expression. *Tremendum* suggested an overwhelming awe in response to God's infused transcendence.

No matter how ingenious, no matter how descriptive, no matter how breathtaking a statement about God may be, it does not reveal the relational presence of *Thou*. Who God really is will always outdistance solitary attempts to understand God. God's *mysterium tremendum* is the simultaneous presence of transcendence and immanence.

SMITH, 79 *MYSTERIUM TREMENDUM*	KAUFMANN, 127–28 *MYSTERIUM TREMENDUM*
Men do not find God if they stay in the world. They do not find Him if they leave the world. He who goes out with his whole being to meet his *Thou* and carries to it all being that is in the world, finds Him who cannot be sought.	One does not find God if one remains in the world; one does not find God if one leaves the world. Whoever goes forth to his You with his whole being and carries to it all the being of the world, finds him whom one cannot seek.
Of course, God is the "wholly Other"; but he is also the wholly Same, the wholly Present. Of course He is the *Mysterium Tremendum* that appears and overthrows; but He is also the mystery of the self-evident, nearer to me than my *I*.	Of course, God is "the wholly other"; but he is also the wholly same: the wholly present. Of course, he is the *mysterium tremendum* that appears and overwhelms; but he is also the mystery of the obvious that is closer to me than my own I.
If you explore the life of things and of conditioned being you come to the unfathomable, if you deny the life of things and of conditioned being you stand before nothingness, if you hallow this life you meet the living God.	When you fathom the life of things and of conditionality, you reach the indissoluble; when you dispute the life of things and of conditionality, you wind up before the nothing; when you consecrate life you encounter the living God.

God expresses a unity of presence in which the transcendent manifests the immanent and the immanent also manifests the transcendent. In a sentence, God is the immediate presence of the "wholly Other" who *happen*s in every genuine relationship with nature, with persons, and with spirit becoming forms, and who creates, reveals, and redeems through each unique relational act.

Divine-Human Partnership

God is always, according to Buber, ready to enter into a partnership with anyone who turns with their whole being toward the unknown God. We might imagine turning to someone like the perfect listener: someone who not only hears every word but also hears our thoughts, even those we are not yet aware of; someone who completely understands what we mean by everything that we say and don't say; and someone who always responds honestly, compassionately, and justly.

To focus even more clearly on the way we perceive and misperceive God, Buber moves, in Part III of *I and Thou,* back to the subject of feelings and our human tendency to become feeling-oriented. For Buber, feelings are part of the soul's dynamics and exist in polar tension to each other (love-hate, pleasure-displeasure, and so on). Feelings are conditioned by their opposites and are relativized by personal psychologies. It is clear, for Buber, that God cannot be reduced to a feeling, even to a "feeling of absolute dependence." At the same time, Buber suggests that we know in our heart that we need God even though we do not know that God needs us:

SMITH, 82 "GOD WHO BECOMES"	KAUFMANN, 130 "THE EMERGING GOD"
You know always in your heart that you need God more than everything; but do you not know too that God needs you—in the fullness of His eternity needs you?	That you need God more than anything, you know at all times in your heart. But don't you know also that God needs you—in the fullness of his eternity, you?

How would man be, how would you be, if God did not need him, did not need you? You need God, in order to be—and God needs you, for the very meaning of your life. In instruction and in poems men are at pains to say more, and they say too much—what turgid and presumptuous talk that is about the "God who becomes"; but we know unshakeably in our hearts that there is a becoming of a God that is. The world is not divine sport, it is divine destiny. There is a divine meaning in the life of the world, of man, of human persons, of you and of me.

How would man exist if God did not need him, and how would you exist? You need God in order to be, and God needs you—for that which is the meaning of your life. Teachings and poems try to say more, and say too much: how murky and presumptuous is the chatter of "the emerging God"—but the emergence of the living God we know unswervingly in our hearts. The world is not divine play, it is divine fate. That there are world, man, the human person, you and I, has divine meaning.

Rather than dependence, Buber speaks of partnership—of a need for the "other" that exists on both sides of the divine-human relationship. It is the *partnership* with the "eternal *Thou*" that makes possible every meaningful relation to the world. Since the "eternal *Thou*" is ever becoming new in unique, unrepeatable situations, God can never be tied either to dogmatic formulations or to specific rituals. The mystery cannot be contained in a feeling. The "eternal *Thou*" is a living Presence who can never become an *It*. Nothing limits God. Indeed, God is the ever-present partner throughout all of existence.[2]

Mysticisms of Absorption

Early in his career Buber was deeply influenced by the study of mysticism and mystical experiences, which became a continuing intellectual and spiritual resource for him. In 1899 Buber became acquainted with a group near Berlin called the New Community.

Led and taught by Gustav Landauer, who was later to become one of Buber's closest friends, the New Community provided Buber with an outlet for his mystical encounters.

Five years later, in 1904, at the University of Vienna, Buber completed his doctoral dissertation on the German mystics Nicholas of Cusa and Jakob Boehme. From Nicholas of Cusa, Buber began to incorporate into his thinking an emphasis on the uniqueness of the person and the unique reality that a person encounters. From Jakob Boehme he took the concept that opposites unite without diminishing their opposition. The idea of uniqueness within a kind of unity would eventually enter his this-worldly philosophy, long after he abandoned the mystical quest for the dialogical one.

As he studied the world's mystical texts, Buber gathered and arranged testimonies from mystics of all ages and published them in a book called *Ecstatic Confessions* (1909). Anticipating his basic theme of *I and Thou*, in this book Buber sees everyday life composed of a whirlwind of feelings and objects. Breaking out of these whirlwinds, mystics across religious traditions experience the unity beyond all multiplicities. They probed what Buber called "the most inward of all experience...God's highest gift." Including texts from Pagan, Asian, Gnostic, Eastern Orthodox, Catholic, Protestant, Jewish, and Islamic traditions, Buber orchestrated two motifs: (1) that the ecstatic experience does have a nature of its own; and (2) that there is an unbridgeable gulf between the ecstatic experience and its verbal expression.

But, in 1957, the year that he visited America and met with the psychologist Carl Rogers, Buber published *Pointing the Way*, a selection of essays he had written between 1909 and 1954. In his Foreword to this collection Buber identified the mystical early period of his intellectual life as a stage that he had to pass through before returning to the world. Succinctly, he called that temporary stage an "absorption" into the "all-absorbing unity of own self" (ix), in which "the great dialogue between I and Thou is silent; nothing else exists than self" (x).

However persuasive mystical thinking was in his early formation, Buber later reevaluated the significance of mysticisms East and West, partly as a result of the war, partly through his study of

Hasidism, but mostly in response to life-altering encounters. Indeed, while much of Buber's early thought is grounded in mysticism, his life's work can be viewed as a movement from mysticism to a philosophy of dialogue. He never entirely discarded the most prominent first influences on his early thinking. Hinduism, Buddhism, Taoism, and German Romanticism were never entirely absent from his way of thinking.

By the time he wrote *I and Thou* Buber critiqued several types of mysticism. In forms of Hindu mysticism, for instance, the "I" is seen to collapse and become one with God. In this I-less form of realization God draws us into ecstasies that send us outside ourselves, or else enters into us, as it were, "from the inside," and overtakes us. Though each experience begins in a polarity of partners—God and the self—it ends in their identity. This happens, for instance, in the common Hindu and Buddhist logical paradox: I am I and Thou art I. Buber translated this into the dialogically impossible formulation: "The I is the *Thou*, the *Thou* is the I." For Buber, the subject-other positions essential to genuine dialogue are annihilated in the fusion of self and Other when mystics speak in these terms. Buber equally understood that these were just terms and necessarily fell short of describing the mystical experience.

Buber's critique of mysticisms is based on the objection that these identity-positions eliminate the possibility of real meeting. In the Hindu view one partner swallows up the other; in the Zen tradition the necessary polarity of "I" and "God" is ultimately overcome in non-duality. In both cases the unity that is attained is attained within itself, or within one's "self." These forms of mystical unification and transformation are situated in an illusion of the human spirit that is bent back on itself. In mysticism generally, the truly "human" is said to occur within *the* self, where the "eternal *Thou*" is said to reside. Buber rejects the Hindu and Buddhist views because "both abolish relation" between this self and others (Smith, 84).[3]

Eternal Presence

After describing the *Mysterium Tremendum* and critiquing mysticism from the perspective of his dialogical anthropology,

Buber returns his attention to the realms of relationship introduced in Chapter 2 in order to extend the idea that in each relational sphere, through every particular *Thou,* we "address the eternal *Thou.*"

SMITH, 101
THE ONE PRESENT

KAUFMANN, 150
THE ONE PRESENCE

In every sphere in its own way, through each process of becoming that is present to us, we look out toward the fringe of the eternal *Thou;* in each we are aware of a breath from the eternal *Thou;* in each *Thou* we address the eternal *Thou.*

Every sphere is compassed in the eternal *Thou,* but it is not compassed in them.

Through every sphere shines the one present.

In every sphere, in every relational act, through everything that becomes present to us, we gaze toward the train of the eternal You; in each we perceive a breath of it; in every You we address the eternal You, in every sphere according to its manner. All spheres are included in it, while it is included in none.

Through all of them shines the one presence.

Both Smith and Kaufmann here evoke different but valid elements of Buber's meaning.[4] Where Smith uses "one present" to describe the "eternal *Thou,*" Kaufmann changes the adjective to a noun, "one presence." They agree that "the one" shines. But for Smith, it is "the one [who is] present." For Kaufmann, "the one" is the presence itself. Buber's meaning is closer to a compromise: God is the one presence who is always present and always shines.

Here, Buber casts his earlier discussion of the three relational realms in an intriguing new image: in each genuine relationship we can glimpse the "fringe of the eternal *Thou.*" The realm of the between opens up to the realm of the transcendent. In *Eclipse of God* Buber writes: "The religious reality of the meeting with the Meeter, who shines through all forms and is Himself formless, knows no image of Him, nothing comprehensible as object. It knows only the presence of the Present One" (45). God is an ever-becoming, ever-present partner in creation, who always listens and responds. In each particular *Thou* we are addressed by, and in turn address, the eternal partner who responds to our address as we respond to God through the other.[5]

Ich Bin Da

One of the difficulties confronting Buber here is that while human thought contains multiple descriptions of God, none is God's own. True, the scriptures are replete with "revealed," or "inspired," or "envisioned" depictions of God. Yet these descriptions are not self-designations. There is, however, one place in scripture where it is said that God speaks a name. In the Book of Exodus (3:13–15), when Moses asks for God's name at the burning bush on Mt. Sinai, God's answer is usually translated as "I am who I am" or "I am here as I am." In the revised edition of *I and Thou* Buber inserted a significant adjustment to his and most translations of God's self-revelation:

SMITH, 111–12
ETERNAL REVELATION

This is the eternal revelation that is present here and now. I know of no revelation and believe in none whose primal phenomenon is not precisely this. I do not believe in a self-naming of God, a self-definition of God before men. The Word of revelation is *I am that I am.* That which reveals is that which reveals. That which is *is,* and nothing more. The eternal source of strength streams, the eternal contact persists, the eternal voice sounds forth, and nothing more.

KAUFMANN, 160
ETERNAL REVELATION

This is the eternal revelation which is present in the here and now. I neither know of nor believe in any revelation that is not the same in its primal phenomenon. I do not believe in God's naming himself or in God's defining himself before man. The word of revelation is: I am there as whoever I am there. That which reveals is that which reveals. That which has being is there, nothing more. The eternal source of strength flows, the eternal touch is waiting, the eternal voice sounds, nothing more.

The key self-description of God in the Hebrew Bible—*Ehyeh asher ehyeh*—Buber renders into the German *"Ich bin da."* *Da* can mean "here" or "there" or "present." In the 1923 first edition of *I and Thou* Buber's emphasis was on the German pronoun *"der"* which means "the one." However, while working with Rosenzweig on their translation of the Bible, Buber shifted his emphasis to God's present-ness or "here-ness."

EXODUS 3:14 IN I AND THOU

1923 version (p. 112)	1957 version (p. 112)
"Ich bin der, der ich bin."	"Ich bin da als der ich da bin."
"I am the one, who I am."	"I am here as the one who is present."

Rather than a name, God gives eternal presence, as Kaufmann's translation reveals: "I am there as whoever I am there" (Kaufmann, 160). In his study *Moses: The Revelation and the Covenant,* Buber rejects Smith's use of the usual translation "I am that I am." In its place Buber offers "happening, coming into being, being there, being present" (52).

Commenting on the Genesis verse in *On the Bible,* Buber writes that God's use of *ehyeh* means "I shall be," and "I am present," and "I shall be present" (54, 60). What God said in response to Moses, then, was "I am present as the one who is fully and unconditionally present." In other words, the "eternal *Thou*" is the One who will be present in each moment that God's presence is sought. God's self-comprehension, for Buber, includes all pasts and all futures, and all three realms of dialogue.

Ordinarily Holy

The essence of God's revelation is expressed in *I and Thou* by two interrelated attributes: (1) *transcendent presence* of all beings, and (2) *immanent presence* without absence of the One who always listens and always responds. To emphasize this interrelated realization, it is helpful to review and compare what Buber says about "God" in both the first edition of *I and Thou* and in the "Postscript" (the following passages are taken from Smith's translation):

"GOD" IN *I AND THOU*

• "Every particular *Thou* is a glimpse through to the eternal *Thou;* by means of every particular *Thou* the primary word addresses the eternal *Thou.*" (75)

• "God is the 'wholly Other'; but He is also the 'wholly Same,' the 'wholly Present.' Of course he is the *Mysterium Tremendum* that appears and overthrows; but He is also the mystery of the self-evident, nearer to me than my *I.*" (79)

• "If you hallow this life you meet the living God." (79)

• "There is no such thing as seeking God, for there is nothing in which He could not be found." (80)

• "You know always in your heart that you need God more than everything; but do you not know too that God needs you—in the fullness of His eternity needs you?" (82)

• "The relation with man is the real simile of the relation with God; in it true address receives true response; except that in God's response everything, the universe, is made manifest as language." (103)

• "[The eternal *Thou*] can be found neither in nor out of the world; for it cannot be experienced, or thought; for we miss Him, Him who is, if we say 'I believe that He is'—'He' is also a metaphor, but 'Thou' is not." (112)

• "[God is 'wholly Other,' 'wholly Same,' 'wholly Present']: the eternal source of strength streams, the eternal contact persists, the eternal voice sounds forth, and nothing more." (112)

"GOD" IN THE "POSTSCRIPT"

• "The description of God as a Person is indispensable for everyone who like myself means by 'God' not a principle as I do, him who...: but who rather means by 'God'...enters into a direct relation[ship] with us men in creative, revealing, and redeeming acts, and thus makes it possible for us to enter into a direct relation[ship] with him." (135)

• "God's speech to men penetrates what happens in the life of each one of us, and all that happens in the world around us, biographical and historical, and makes it for you and me into instruction, message, demand." (136)

143

Throughout these remarks the "eternal *Thou*" is expressed through two interrelated attributes. The *transcendence* of God, the "wholly Other," is the Source of all being. The *immanence* of God, the "wholly Same" and "wholly Present," needs humans just as humans need God. The immanence of God is further exemplified in the "Postscript" as the "absolute Person" who brings the fullness of meaning into the world.[6] The dialogical God is everywhere "wholly Present."

> God says to man, as he said to Moses: "Put off thy shoes from thy feet"—Put off the habitual which encloses your foot, and you will know that the place on which you are now standing is holy ground. (*Tales of the Hasidim,* 132)

This very place, where God is present, is holy.

Figure 5–2 distinguishes the "eternal *Thou*" of *I and Thou* and the "absolute Person" of the "Postscript."

Figure 5–2. The "Eternal Thou*" as the "Absolute Person"*

I AND THOU (1923)

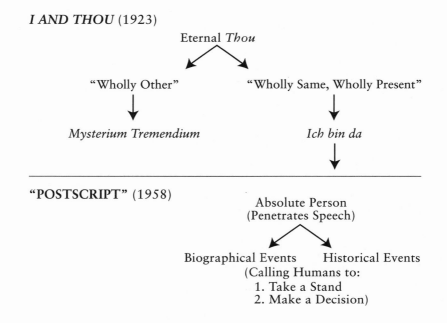

Eternal *Thou*

"Wholly Other"   "Wholly Same, Wholly Present"

Mysterium Tremendium   *Ich bin da*

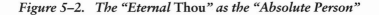

"POSTSCRIPT" (1958)

Absolute Person
(Penetrates Speech)

Biographical Events   Historical Events
(Calling Humans to:
1. Take a Stand
2. Make a Decision)

Absolute Person

The image of God as "absolute Person" in the last pages of the "Postscript" to *I and Thou* is one of Buber's most significant contributions to theological thought. Buber's shift in emphasis to the "absolute Person" brings attention to, and characterizes, the immanence-presence dimension of the "eternal *Thou*." In no way, however, does Buber limit God to any particular image, let alone to the image of God as "Person." As Maurice Friedman writes in *Martin Buber and the Eternal*: "God is the Absolute Person who *is* not a person but *becomes* one, so to speak, to love and be loved, to know and be known by us" (44).

An obvious question at this point: Why did Buber find it necessary to add another description, the "absolute Person," to his image of the "eternal *Thou*"? Buber's twofold response to another question, one frequently asked by early readers of *I and Thou*, suggests Buber's response to this question. How can the "eternal *Thou*" be at the same time "exclusive and inclusive" of all human relationships? (Smith, 134). That is, "How can the *Thou*-relationship" between a person and God "include all other *I-Thou* relation[ship]s of this man?" (Smith, 134).

Over the years Buber noticed that many readers and interpreters of *I and Thou* tended to respond to both of these questions by reducing the "eternal *Thou*" to a philosophical or theological concept. It therefore became indispensable for Buber to describe God as "a Person"—indeed, "the absolute Person; that is, the person who cannot be limited" (Smith, 136). The attribute "absolute Person" emphasizes God's immediacy, God's "inclusiveness." A person's *Thou*-relationship to God thus includes and embraces all other *I-Thou* relationships.

By adding the attribute of "Person" to his description of God, Buber signifies the generative dynamic of interhuman relationships and articulates the dynamics of how God communicates with humans. First, as "Person" God enters into direct relationship with us in creative, revealing, and redeeming acts and makes it possible for us to enter direct relationships with God and with others. Second, as "Person" God addresses us by penetrating the biographical and historical life events that shape us with instruction, message, and the demand that we take a stand.

As the "absolute Person" God's eternal presence draws near and is reflected through every genuine relationship. In a remarkably revealing comment in *Philosophical Interrogations,* Buber writes that in order to enter into relationship with humans, "God has put on himself 'the servant's garment of the person'" (91). Buber chooses the term *Person* because it embodies the significance of the relationship between personal and external life. At the same time Buber asserts that God is "Person" only in dialogue with human beings. That is, God's being "absolute Person" is our doorway to God's service to humankind.

SMITH, 135
GOD AS A PERSON

KAUFMANN, 180–81
GOD AS A PERSON

The description of God as Person is indispensable for everyone who like myself means by "God" not a principle...and like myself means by "God" not an idea...: but who rather means by "God," as I do, him who—whatever else he may be—enters into a direct relation with us men in creative, revealing and redeeming acts, and thus makes it possible for us to enter into a direct relation with him. This ground and meaning of our existence constitutes a mutuality, arising again and again, such as can subsist only between persons. The concept of personal being is indeed completely incapable of declaring what God's essential being is, but it is both permitted and necessary to say that God is *also* a Person.

The designation of God as a person is indispensable for all who, like myself, do not mean a principle when they say "God,"...and who, like myself, do not mean an idea when they say "God"...—all who, like myself, mean by "God" him that, whatever else he may be in addition, enters into a direct relationship to us human beings through creative, revelatory, and redemptive acts, and thus makes it possible for us to enter into a direct relationship to him. This ground and meaning of our existence establishes each time a mutuality of the kind that can obtain only between persons. The concept of personhood is, of course, utterly incapable of describing the nature of God; but it is permitted and necessary to say that God is *also* a person.

"It is as the absolute Person that God enters into direct relation[ship] with us" (Smith, 136).[7] God speaks personally (in
Buber's sense of "person"), but God is not a person in any finite
way. The person who turns to God, Buber reminds us, "need not
turn away from any other *I-Thou* relation[ship]"; rather, these are
"fulfilled 'in the face of God'" (Smith, 136). The metaphor of God
as "absolute Person" does not mean an objective idea that one
holds. Rather, as Buber writes in *Eclipse of God,*

> it is indeed legitimate to speak of the person of God within the
> religious relation and in its language; but in so doing we are
> making no statement about the Absolute which reduces it to
> the personal. We are rather saying that it enters into the rela-
> tionship as the Absolute Person whom we call God. (96–97)

God's Speaking Voice

For Buber, God is the nearest One, the always ready, supreme
partner in dialogue. God addresses us by standing directly, nearly,
and lastingly with us as the eternal partner who is always ready to
become dialogically present. Yet, we might ask, doesn't dialogue
require each partner to speak? And what type of mutuality exists
between human beings and God? In the "Postscript" to *I and Thou,*
the "eternal *Thou,*" who may properly only be addressed and not
expressed, meets us as the "absolute Person." Buber writes:

SMITH, 136–37 GOD'S SPEECH	KAUFMANN, 182 GOD'S ADDRESS
God's speech to men pene-trates what happens in the life of each one of us, and all that happens in the world around us, biographical and histori-cal, and makes it for you and me into instruction, message, demand. Happening upon happening, situation upon situation, are enabled and empowered by the personal	God's address to man pene-trates the events in all our lives and all the events in the world around us, everything biographical and everything historical, and turns it into instruction, into demands for you and me. Event upon event, situation upon situa-tion is enabled and empow-ered by this personal language

147

speech of God to demand of the human person that he take his stand and make his decision. Often enough we think there is nothing to hear, but long before we have ourselves put wax in our ears.

The existence of mutuality between God and man cannot be proved, just as God's existence cannot be proved.

to call upon the human person to endure and decide. Often we think that there is nothing to be heard as if we had not long ago plugged wax into our own ears.

The existence of mutuality between God and man cannot be proved any more than the existence of God.

Accordingly, God's speaking penetrates through every genuine interhuman relationship, especially when the words of others stand out as "instruction, message, demand."[8] When turning to God with unreserved spontaneity, I bring all other relationships before God, to be transformed in God's presence. Our conversations with God and God's conversation with us happen not only alongside of the everyday but also penetrate into our lived reality. In event upon event, happening upon happening, the personal address of God, through others, enables us to take a stand, to make decisions, and to continue in a direction of movement.[9]

Divine *Shekinah*

In *The Way of Man* Buber relates several stories from the Hasidic tradition that illustrate God's "way" of speaking to us. Once, the story goes, Rabbi Pinhas was told of the great misery among the needy. He listened in grief. Then, he responded: "Let us draw God into the world and all need will be quenched" (40). But is it possible, Buber wonders, to bring God down to earth? By way of an answer to this pertinent question, Buber refers to another story in which the same rabbi poses this question to his community: "Where is the dwelling of God?" This question surprised a number of learned men who happened to be visiting the rabbi. They laughed. "What a thing to ask! Is not the whole world full of

God's glory?" Then the Rabbi of Kotzk answered his own question: "God dwells wherever man lets him in" (41).

So, the ultimate purpose of life, Buber writes, at least according to these stories, is that God becomes manifest in the world whenever we let God in. But we let God in only where we really stand, where we actually live. As we maintain intercourse with the world entrusted to us, we help the holy divine presence to accomplish itself in that place. In other words, we establish, in this place, a dwelling for the divine *shekinah,* the glory of God, immanent in the world. Buber affirms this point in *On Judaism:*

> We ought to understand that to "realize God" means to prepare the world for God, as a place for His reality—to help the world become God-real...; it means, in other and sacred words, to make reality one. This is our service in the Kingdom's becoming. (9)

What Buber indicates here is a vibrant connection between moments of relationship with the world and the presence of the "eternal *Thou.*" Addressing and being addressed by the "eternal *Thou*" finally is grounded in trust *(emunah).*

Dialogue begins with the trust that, in particular situations or occasions, there will be genuine responses. Trust cannot be induced by auto-suggestion. One needs to take risks, to remain open to graces coming from the relationship. Trusting in God, for Buber, is not based on desiring what God can do for us. Rather, unconditional trust enables us, as long as we have the strength, to go forth to meet the one whom Buber glimpsed in a poem, "Elijah," as "eternally complete, soft and motherly."

The Alone to the Alone

The "absolute *Thou*" confronts me, and at the same time I step into an immediate relationship with God, both through others and directly as "the alone to the Alone." This relationship is one of being *chosen* and of *choosing,* an activity of the whole person. Buber calls this activity a doing-less doing, in which a person is not agitated by anything of a partial nature. Again, it is easy to hear traces of Buber's interest in Taoism here, especially in its teaching of "letting go," or *wu-wei*. Finally, according to Buber, I relate to God neither through my own effort nor without it.

Maurice Friedman once asked Buber another intriguing question: "Is God loved *only* through man and never apart from him?" Various religious traditions speak tirelessly of entering into a direct relationship with God. Therefore, Friedman's question concerned the necessity, or lack thereof, for a mediating agency. Were these "personal God" religions correct? In *Philosophical Interrogations* Buber explains:

> When I speak of the exclusion of the world from the relation to God, I do not speak of the *hour* of man, but of his *life*. I regard it as unqualifiably legitimate when a man again and again, in an hour of religious fervor, adoring and praying, enters into a direct, "world-free" relation to God; and my heart understands as well the Byzantine composer of hymns who speaks as "the alone to the Alone," as also that Hasidic rabbi who, feeling himself a stranger on earth, asks God, who is also, indeed, a stranger on earth, to grant him, just for that reason, his friendship. But a "life with God" erected on the rejection of the living is no life with God. Often we hear of animals who have been loved by holy hermits, but I would not be able to regard anyone as holy who in the desert ceased to love the men whom he had left. (85–86)

Buber's eye-opening distinction between the "hour" and the "life" of humans is based on the double insight that (1) through relating to persons we relate to God, and (2) through our relationships God addresses us unconditionally both *inclusively* (for we are included in God's presence) and *exclusively* (in the exclusive uniqueness of our own ground of being). Even the hour of deeply motivated prayer to the divine Presence—"the alone to the Alone"— is followed by hours of lived reality with others—a life that God creates, through which God reveals, and which God redeems.

Meetings

Question and Answer

It was in May of the year 1914 (my wife and I and our two children, now had already lived some eight years in a suburb of Berlin) when Reverend Hechler, whom I had not seen for a long time, called me. He was just in Berlin and would like to visit me. Soon afterward he came....

Hechler stayed a few hours with us. Then I accompanied him to the railway station. In order to get there, one first had to go to the end of the small street of the "colony" in which we lived and then on a narrow path covered with coal-dust, the so-called "black path" along the railroad tracks. When we had reached the corner where the colony street met this path, Hechler stood still, placed his hand on my shoulder and said: "Dear friend! We live in a great time. Tell me: Do you believe in God?" It was a while before I answered, then I reassured the old man as best I could: He need have no concern about me in this matter. Upon this I brought him to the railway station and installed him in his train.

When I now returned home, however, and again came to that corner where the black path issued into our street, I stood still. I had to ponder to the depths of the matter. Had I said the truth? Did I "believe" in the God whom Hechler meant? What was the case with me? I stood a long time on the corner determined not to go further before I had found the right answer.

Suddenly in my spirit, there where speech again and again forms itself, there arose without having been formulated by me, word for word distinct:

"If to believe in God means to be able to talk about him in the third person, then I do not believe in God. If to believe in him means to be able to talk to him, then I believe in God." And after a while further: "The God who gives Daniel such foreknowledge of this hour of human history, this hour before the 'world war,' that its fixed place in the march of the ages can be foredetermined, is not my God and not God. The God to whom Daniel prays in his suffering is my God and the God of all."

I remained standing for a long while on the corner of the black path and gave myself up to the clarity, now beyond speech, that had begun. (42–44)

Notice the difference between Buber's first and his second response to Hechler's question. First, Buber assured Hechler that he need not be concerned about the matter of belief in God. But then, Buber pondered the question again. Notice that after Buber stood for a long time by himself, "there arose without having been formulated by me" the right answer.

And notice that when Buber mentions that he does not *believe* in God, he means the fictive God who is conditioned by his own perceptions and projections. That is, "if to believe in God means to be able to talk about him in the third person," Buber would rather not speak of God. Hitherto, God had been the impersonal Godhead in the soul of the solitary mystic. But, if "to believe in him means to be able to talk to him, then I believe in God." Again, Buber's emphasis remains on the *presentness* of God.

Practice Exercises

While the following questions suggest specific avenues of writing, thinking, and pondering, you may simply wish to reflect on a particular passage in *I and Thou* from this chapter and then (1) write about your dialogue with this passage, and (2) discuss your responses in dialogue with others.

1. If I choose to live dialogue, how (in what ways) do I glimpse the "eternal *Thou*"?

2. For Buber, prayer is a speaking to God that ultimately asks for the divine Presence to become dialogically perceivable. How might Buber describe prayer?

3. Who is God for you? How does God relate to the world? More specifically, how does God communicate with you? Or does God communicate with you at all?

4. Who is God for Buber? How does Buber know God? How does God speak to Buber? In this context how do you respond to Buber's understanding of God? And how do you think Buber would respond to your response?

5. While Buber's philosophy of dialogue grew from genuine meetings, he sometimes described it in religious terms. Do you think that genuine dialogue depends on this belief structure, or could it be grounded as well in secular belief?

6. How would you have answered Hechler's question? Comment on the significance of Buber's answer: (1) its origin; (2) its interpretation; and (3) its implications.

Notes

1. It is important not to differentiate between Smith's punctuation and Kaufmann's punctuation. For Smith, "God is the 'wholly Other'; but He is also the wholly Same, the wholly Present." This punctuation is not meant to suggest that there are three elements or characteristics of God: "wholly Other," "wholly Same," "wholly Present." This punctuation is not present in the German text. Kaufmann writes that God is "the wholly other; but he is also the wholly same: the wholly present." In each translation, the "wholly present" is a further exemplification of the "wholly same." In other words, Buber evokes a double order of presence: the immanent and the transcendent.

2. Buber talks about "presumptuous chatter of the 'God who becomes'" (Smith), and the "emerging God" (Kaufmann). Here, Buber means the becoming of the living God that happens only in relationship. Therefore, Kaufmann's translation should read: "but the *becoming* of the living God."

3. By extending his critique of mysticism to a kind of relational mysticism, he took a step beyond his early studies. He writes: "What the ecstatic calls unification is the rapturous dynamics of the relationship....The relationship itself in its vital unity is felt so vehemently that its members pale in the process" (Kaufmann, 135). This passage appears in the context of a discussion of Eros, in which people "are so enraptured by the miracle of the embrace that their knowledge of *I* and *Thou* perishes in the feeling of a unity that does not and cannot exist" (Smith, 87). Instead, the "dynamics of relationship" span a continuum of behavioral patterns.

In a few cases, at least, a "vital unity" may be said to embrace both *I* and *Thou,* who are, in a sense, temporally "not there." Later, in *Philosophical Interrogations* Buber writes: "No matter how all-embracing the relation of two beings to each other may be, it does not in any sense mean their 'unification'" (27), though in some moments a vital relational unity may become lifted up in which *I* and *Thou* are temporarily forgotten. In such an event, while a person is brought outside of self-consciousness, one does not give up one's stand in the moment. Having spoken of the fringe of the relational continuum, Buber returns us to "the central reality of everyday earthly hour with its sun breaking on a maple twig and the intimation of the eternal *Thou*" (Smith, 89).

4. Kaufmann's translation is correct. Smith leaves out "in every relational act." Buber always uses the personal pronoun for the "eternal *Thou*." Therefore, the passage should read: "All spheres are included in *him* while *he* is included in none."

5. On March 12, 1922, Buber presented the last of a series of lectures called "Religion as Presence" (contained in *Buber's Way to "I and Thou"*), which would become an oral preview of entire sections of *I and Thou*: "With the eternal presence, the eternal presentness of God, man is entering-into-relation[ship], over and over, with this eternal presence" (122). Merely mentally reflecting back upon oneself, on the other hand, again and again turns the living God into an object of thought. In *The Philosophy of Martin Buber*, Buber adds, "Even when he is not able to turn to God with collected soul, God's presence, the presence of his eternal Thou, is primally real" (705).

6. Most immediately, God is apprehended, not comprehended, through the spirit of the "between." As Robert Wood notes in *Martin Buber's Ontology*: "In the I-Thou relation the Between comes into being as such: spirit appears in the world and fills it with meaning. Presence is deepened [and] opens up to...the Transcendent" (115). In keeping with the Hasidic tradition, Buber affirmed that God's transcendence remains concealed, yet God's presence becomes manifest as each unique particular becomes most real. In other words, to open ourselves to the "wholly Other" does not mean to transcend the world but to discover transcendence in the "ordinarily holy." Each living moment can become sacramental.

7. Significantly, Buber included a very important paragraph in the "Postscript" (which was left out of the original 1958 edition because it arrived at the publishers too late to be included). In that paragraph Buber begins: "As a Person God gives personal life, he makes us as persons capable of meeting with him and with one another" (Smith, 136). The paragraph concludes: "The man who turns to him [God] therefore need not turn away from any other *I-Thou* relation[ship]; but he properly brings them to him, and lets them be fulfilled 'in the face of God'" (Smith, 136).

Smith's translation—"creative, revealing and redeeming acts"—is much closer to the German text. Smith's participles evoke the movement of *change* that is always important for Buber. By using nouns such as "revelatory and redemptive acts," Kaufmann freezes the movement. Kaufmann correctly translates the German term *"das Wesen Gottes"* as "the nature of God."

8. Both Smith's translation ("instruction, message, demand...") and Kaufmann's translation ("instructions, into demands...") are incorrect. Buber uses the word *Weisung,* which means "pointing toward" or "giving direction." The text should read: "and makes it for you and me as a pointer, as request." Buber uses words that express a dynamic openness to change and development. The German text uses the word *erheischen,* which means "to call forth." The text should read: "to call forth from the person taking a stand and deciding...."

9. At the center of biblical Judaism, for Buber, is the dialogue between God and humans. In "The Dialogue Between Heaven and Earth," in *On Judaism,* Buber provides two striking passages that depict the dynamics and the parameters of this relationship:

> Transcendence speaks to our hearts at the essential moments of personal life. And there is a language in which we can answer it; it is the language of our actions and attitudes, our reactions and our abstentions. (216)

He continues later in the chapter:

> God speaks not only to the individual and to the community, within the limits and under the conditions of a particular biographical or historical situation. Everything, being and becoming, nature and history, is essentially a divine pronouncement *[Aussprache],* an infinite context of signs meant to be perceived and understood by perceiving and understanding creatures. (221)

We do our part by paying attention to those surprise moments arising in dialogical conversations in which our anxieties and sufferings are addressed, either directly or indirectly, for instance, by something that is said which takes on a divine accent. This may come simply as a question—for example, What will you put up with? or Have you fully explained yourself?—or as a line of poetry like "fair forward."

Chapter 6

The Way of "Turning"

Turning is the recognition of the Centre and the act
of turning again to it. In this act of the being the
buried relational power of man rises again, the wave
that carries all the spheres of relation swells in living
streams to give new life to our world.

By now, it is clear that the structure of Buber's book, and
ours, radiates from a central unity that unifies Buber's two primal
word pairs *(I-Thou* and *I-It)* and his basic relational realms. Each
chapter embodies and reflects this central design. Part II (Chapters 3 and 4) provides two interhuman consequences of the Generating Grid, and Part III (Chapters 5 and 6) provides two
underlying foundations of the *I and Thou* Grid. In the last chapter
we focused on one of these foundations, the transcendent realm.
We can summarize Buber's understanding of the transcendent
realm by saying that

- extended lines of relationship meet in the "eternal *Thou*";

- every particular *Thou* is a glimpse through to the "eternal
  Thou";

- the "inborn *Thou*" is realized in each relationship and
  consummated in none;

- God is the "wholly Other"; but God is also the "wholly Same," the "wholly Present";

- God is the *mysterium tremendum* who is also the mystery of the self-evident; and

- God is not an idea, but the "absolute Person" always ready to enter into direct relationship, always listening, always responding.

While connected to Chapter 5—as an underlying, foundational interaction of the Generating Grid—this chapter qualifies the whole book. The act of "turning" (away from personal willfulness and toward relationship) is fundamentally present in the activation of each dimension of genuine dialogue. As Buber's interrelated insights continue bearing meaningful fruit, one begins practicing them through acts of turning. Following the direction of Buber's thought in this chapter, and in the "Postscript," our reading along with Buber's book begins to become more practice oriented.

A Bridge

In the context of Buber's life work, his 1913 book *Daniel: Dialogues on Realization* formed a bridge between his earlier mystical orientation and his emerging philosophy of dialogue. It was in Daniel that Buber first introduced his concept of "holy insecurity," which remained central to his understanding of Hasidism and biblical prophecy. The prophets of Israel, Buber writes in the *Eclipse of God* (73),

> always aimed to shatter all security and to proclaim in the opened abyss of the final insecurity the unwished-for God who demands that His human creatures become real…and confounds all who imagine that they can take refuge in the certainty that the temple of God is in their midst.

According to Buber, when human existence becomes shattered by incomprehensible evil, normal security disappears. In the Hasidic tradition, turning to God from the depths of one's soul is born from the despair and the suffering produced by life-shattering events. Yet turning to the unknowable God does not automatically alleviate suffering or guarantee healing. Indeed, the "fear of God," or the "awe of God," expresses the essence of "holy insecurity." For Buber, when a person is most insecure, her or his life expressions become most real. As we will see, turning for Buber was never complete without surrendering to the unfathomable, as well as the personal "claim and responsibility" for every moment.

Unlike many of Buber's key insights, the term *Umkehr* (turning) specifies a practice that is more like an art than like a mystical religion. *Umkehr* refers to the redirecting of one's orientation to life. In his first 1937 translation, Smith rendered the word *Umkehr* with the term "reversal." Unfortunately, "reversal" has several misleading connotations and lacks the crucial biblical overtones contained in Buber's intention.

Therefore, in the 1958 second edition, at the suggestion of Maurice Friedman, Smith retranslated *Umkehr* with the word "turning." Kaufmann, on the other hand, translates *Umkehr* with the word "return." Here, Smith remains closer to Buber's original intention. *Umkehr* is Buber's translation of the Hebrew word *teshuvah,* which denotes a complete turning to God. In this sense, moreover, Buber uses *Umkehr* to indicate the act of turning with one's whole being to meet the other, which implies, at the same time, turning wholly toward God.

The opposite of turning, Buber writes, is "reflexion," bending back on oneself. This backward-bending movement privileges self-consciousness and withdrawal from entering into relationship with others. In other words, by allowing the other to exist only within my own experience, the heart and soul of what is most *human* begins to get lost and dissipates. This happens when I turn my experience inward.

The central importance that Buber attributed to turning toward or outward can be gleaned by paraphrasing its appearances in *I and Thou* (in Smith's translation):

- The most real revelation of all is turning. (57)

- The beginning of turning is when we face the despair of the I emptied of reality. (61)

- The direction of turning arises out of alienation and directs one toward and through surrender. (70)

- To turn is to give up the false self-asserting self, but not to give up the "I," as in mysticism. (78)

- Turning is the recognition of the center, the primal source, and the reawakening of relationship between persons. (100)

- Turning involves a double movement: from solitude and toward the primal source. (101)

- Turning involves a double change: of one's goal and of one's direction of movement. (105)

- The ever-new turning toward relationship is turning to deep bondedness. (116)

- From God's side, turning is called redemption. (120)

Developing the significance of turning, in *Between Man and Man* Buber explained that the basic movement of dialogue is turning toward the other with unreserved spontaneity by opening to an indwelling presence between persons. That is, dialogue is a turning away from a self-reflexive monologue consumed in self-enjoyment and toward the wordless depths of genuine *I-Thou* dialogue. The immediacy of mutuality between persons cannot become present without the graced act of turning toward the uniqueness of the other. "The basic movement of the life of dialogue is *turning* towards the other" (22). Buber develops this theme further in *The Knowledge of Man*:

> In genuine dialogue the turning to the partner takes place in all truth, that is, it is a turning of the being.
> But where the dialogue is fulfilled in its being, between partners who have turned to one another in truth, who express themselves without reserve and are free of the desire

for semblance, there is brought into being a memorable common fruitfulness which is to be found nowhere else. (85, 86)

Unified Elements

In turning one drops facades or the need to seem to be different than one really is. Swinging outward, one turns toward the other person and, in the process, toward "the between," through which the presence of the "eternal *Thou*" can be glimpsed. When turning is mutual, a "memorable common fruitfulness" is brought into existence. Each person stimulates and is stimulated by a meaningful newness that bonds the two.

In both the second and third parts of *I and Thou* Buber returns again and again to the necessity of practicing turning.

SMITH, 78
TURNING

To be sure, this acceptance presupposes that the further a man has wandered in separated being the more difficult is the venture and the more elemental the turning. This does not mean a giving up of, say, the *I*, as mystical writings usually suppose: the *I* is as indispensable to this, the supreme, as to every relation, since relation is only possible between *I* and *Thou*. It is not the *I*, then, that is given up, but that false self-asserting instinct that makes a man flee to the possessing of things before the unreliable, perilous world of relation which has neither density nor duration and cannot be surveyed.

KAUFMANN, 126
RETURN

To be sure, this acceptance involves a heavier risk and a more fundamental return, the further man has lost his way in separation. What has to be given up is not the I, as most mystics suppose: the I is indispensable for any relationship, including the highest, which always presupposes an I and You. What has to be given up is not the I but that false drive for self-affirmation which impels man to flee from the unreliable, unsolid, unlasting, unpredictable, dangerous world of relation into the having of things.

160

What Buber means by separation—a retreat from relationship toward dwelling in one's own experiences—stands as a chief barrier to turning. The more isolated I become, the more "elemental" the need for turning becomes.[1]

By *elemental*, Buber does not mean "subjective," "self-assertive," or "mystical" realization. Rather, the term *elemental*, for Buber, points back to the particularity of the world, to the significance of everyday events. *Elemental* means "formational," "basic," "grounding." Following this line of thinking, every act of turning forms an elemental unity with and in the world.

The unified elements of turning, then, include the following:

- being fully present
- making the other present
- obedient listening
- affirming and confirming
- imagining the other's side
- withholding nothing
- surrendering trustingly
- being willing to change

Relational Grace

Buber's attention to the relational role of the speaking subject, and thus to his or her preliminary act of genuine turning toward dialogue, results in the kind of meaning that streams into our world when we first recognize the "primal Source."

SMITH, 100–101 PRIMAL SOURCE	KAUFMANN, 149 PRIMAL GROUND
Turning is the recognition of the Centre and the act of turning again to it. In this	Return signifies the re-cognition of the center, turning back to it again. In this

161

act of the being the buried relational power of man rises again, the wave that carries all the spheres of relation swells in living streams to give new life to our world.

Perhaps not to our world alone. For this double movement, of estrangement from the primal Source, in virtue of which the universe is sustained in the process of becoming, and of turning towards the primal Source, in virtue of which the universe is released in being...

essential deed man's buried power to relate is resurrected, the wave of all relational spheres surges up in a living flood and renews our world.

Perhaps not only ours. Dimly we apprehend this double movement—that turning away from the primal ground by virtue of which the universe preserves itself in its becoming, and that turning toward that primal ground by virtue of which the universe redeems itself in being...

Genuine turning is described here as receiving "the Centre and...turning again to it." In doing so, we can release a "buried relational power." According to Buber, genuine dialogue is impossible without prior turning, without shifting from willfulness and self-attention toward interhuman meeting, toward the "central *Thou*" of common mutuality. That is, prior to entering genuine dialogue a person shifts his or her stand wholly toward the other, and in the process toward "the primal Source."

Recall that for Buber turning to dialogue, to genuine meeting, is the central relational event. Turning from selfishness and toward genuine dialogue happens through and results in relational grace. Recall also that "grace" and "will" are equally important sources of genuine dialogue. But this grace, this source, does not come from somewhere else. It is not external to the dialogue. Rather, relational grace refers to the spirit of the "between" that arises from, generates, and supports genuine interhuman meetings.

Figure 6–1. The Central Relational Event

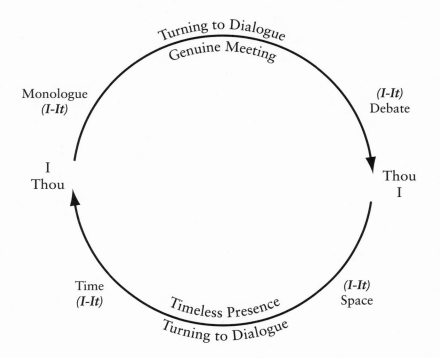

Turning to Dialogue
Genuine Meeting

Monologue
(I-It)

(I-It)
Debate

I
Thou

Thou
I

Time
(I-It)

(I-It)
Space

Timeless Presence
Turning to Dialogue

Double Movement

For Buber, moreover, acts of turning stream through all of the spheres of existence and renew the world. In fact, turning is a double movement: First, in dialogue we turn *away from* everything that would prevent us from entering into genuine relationship with the other; and second, we turn *toward* whoever or whatever presents itself to us. In other words, the double movement requires turning away from self-preoccupation and toward entering-into-relationship. In our lives there is always, writes Buber, a "special something" that takes center stage. Whether that special something is an object of enjoyment or principle of belief, it can frustrate the essential movement of turning.

One of the most common barriers to turning, in Buber's opinion, is the persistent human belief in fate. Examples of fate include a strong belief in survival of the fittest, the law of instincts, social process, dialectical materialism, and cultural cycles. By putting fate in the center of human actions, we leave a human being with little possibility for liberation, and devalue both human will and (more importantly) the relational grace that arises from it. Believing in fate blocks turning:

SMITH, 105	KAUFFMAN, 154
DOUBLE CHANGE	DOUBLE CHANGE
He who is dominated by the idol that he wishes to win, to hold, and to keep—possessed by a desire for possession— has no way to God but that of turning, which is a change not only of goal but also of the nature of his movement.	Whoever is dominated by the idol whom he wants to acquire, have, and hold, possessed by his desire to possess, can find a way to God only by returning, which involves a change not only of the goal but also of the kind of movement.

We can fairly assume that a belief in fate (social Darwinism, for example) exemplifies yet another mental idol akin to the idols we worship whenever we construct and elevate any image of higher power.

But this does not mean that we are called only to change our inner attitudes and destroy these idols. We are called to swing away from being doubled-back upon ourselves, and this means changing our very self-orientation. When we are "possessed by a desire for possession," we become immersed in the world of *It* regardless of what kind of idols we construct to justify this position. Swinging outward toward the other, toward "the between" through which the "eternal *Thou*" is glimpsed, means overcoming this entrapment.

For Buber, this overcoming involves a double movement:

1. Turning *from* separation

   • Giving up self-asserting instincts

   • Abandoning selfish forms of solitude

2. Turning *toward* deep bonding

   • With the world

   • With the primal Source

Turning, in the end, requires practice and mental awareness. Turning *from* separation means giving up self-asserting instincts and abandoning selfish forms of solitude. This style of movement—incessant self-reflexion—reduces God, other humans, and the world into objects of one's own desires. Of course, it is not difficult for most of us to become caught up into thinking about thinking, or to be distracted by distractions, or to need to need.

Deep Bonding

In contrast to self-reflexive behaviors, Buber stresses the need to turn toward a deep bonding with others.

SMITH, 116
TURNING TOWARD
CONNEXION

For the two primary meta-cosmical movements of the world—expansion into its own being and turning to connexion—find their supreme human form, the real spiritual form of their struggle and adjustment, their mingling and separation, in the history of the human relation to God. In turning the Word is born on earth, in expansion the Word enters the chrysalis form of religion, in fresh turning it is born again with new wings.

KAUFMANN, 165
TURNING TOWARD
ASSOCIATION

For the two basic meta-cosmic movements of the world—its expansion into its own being and returning to association [with God]—attain their supreme human form, the true spirit form of their struggle and conciliation, their mixture and separation, in the history of man's relation to God. It is in the return that the word is born on earth; in spreading out it enters the chrysalis of religion; in a new return it is reborn with new wings.

Here Buber indicates the necessity of turning toward *Verbunden-heit,* a somewhat difficult to translate German noun. It comes from the verb *verbinden,* which means "to wrap gauze around an injury." To embrace *verbunden* toward a person means to bind with them in a closely held and healing togetherness.

The Way

At the end of the first edition of *I and Thou,* Buber reflects back upon the path he has followed. Speaking of the Word, of the meaningful speech of revelation, he concludes that "this is the course and the counter-course of the eternal and eternally present Word in history" (Smith, 119).

SMITH, 119–20 HIDDEN *BETWEEN BEINGS*	KAUFMANN, 168 HIDDEN *BETWEEN BEINGS*
But this course is not circular. It is the way. In each new aeon fate becomes more oppressive, turning more shattering. And the theophany becomes ever *nearer,* increasingly near to the sphere that lies *between beings,* to the Kingdom that is hidden in our midst, there between us. History is a mysterious approach. Every spiral of its way leads us both into profounder perversion and more fundamental turning. But the event that from the side of the world is called turning is called from God's side redemption.	But the path is not a circle. It is the way. Doom becomes more oppressive in every new eon, and the return more explosive. And the theophany comes ever *closer,* it comes ever closer to the sphere *between beings—* comes closer to the realm that hides in our midst, in the between. History is a mysterious approach to closeness. Every spiral of its path leads us into deeper corruption and at the same time into more fundamental return. But the God-side of the event whose world-side is called return is called redemption.

Buber moves toward his closing remarks by recalling that the power "to enter into relation[ship] is being buried under increasing objectification" (Smith, 118) in spite of the fact that "God is near His forms if man does not remove them from Him" (Smith,

119). This falling away from and returning to *I-Thou* relationship "is the course and the counter-course of the eternal and eternally present Word in history" (Smith, 119). But the course is not circular. "It is the way" (Smith, 119).

"The way" *(Der Weg)* means, for Buber, the path along which one chooses again and again to go forth into the possibility of deep bonding. It also refers to the behavior of turning without holding oneself back, turning with one's whole existence toward who or what is with us. At the same time, the realization of God's manifestation (theophany) is glimpsed in the sphere that lies between beings. This sphere, central to "the way," Buber writes, often "hides in our midst," in the between, waiting to be disclosed (Kaufmann, 168).

Accordingly, for Buber, history is not simply a cyclic rhythm proceeding in an endless spiral of *I-Thou* and *I-It* consciousness. Rather, it involves an ongoing partnership between humans and the "eternal *Thou*" that expresses itself and is expressed through *creation* (the divine act of building the cosmos), *revelation* (entering into relationship with the transcendent), and *redemption* (the ever-renewed presence of God).[2]

Redemption *(Erlösung),* furthermore, does not simply depend upon God. Buber offers a much more conversational view of history. Each person helps to bring about and to renew the unity of God and the world through genuine relationship. From the midst of the experience of division, an impulse emerges that enables a person to re-enter the world. Redemption from the human side, both personal and historical, involves an ever-renewed willingness, or openness, to risk one's individuality by coming into the presence of "the between." This realm, which Smith translates "Kingdom," is the interhuman bonding of which Buber has spoken from the beginning of *I and Thou*. "The between" is a deep bonding that often, regrettably, remains "hidden in our midst."

"The Way" is discovering the common *humanness* in our midst.

Trust and Redemption

The theological term *redemption,* usually defined from the position of God's subjectivity in relation to human beings, from the human side is received through relational and unconditional trust *(emunah)*. Authentic and clear-sighted trust between person and person renews humanity and redeems history. But involved with unconditional trust is the eternal insecurity associated with meeting the *Thou,* a point that Buber realized quite early through his locked-out relation to his mother. Without unconditional trust, mismeeting and miscommunication are more likely.

But why is trust needed?

If the beginning of dialogue involves turning toward the other, turning itself is made possible by unconditional trust in the other. Whenever we enter into relationship we risk becoming wounded, and we have built up an arsenal of defenses against this danger. Understandably, we fear emotional pain. Therefore, becoming open to being wounded by the other absolutely requires trusting the other. It also involves trusting in the possibility of dialogue itself and in our personal ability to handle emotional pain, whenever it arises.

In *Touchstones of Reality* Friedman describes unconditional trust, which he calls "existential trust," through a Buberian lens in the context of dialogue and meeting. In summary, Friedman makes these points:

- Dialogue begins with trust in existence that enables us to live from moment to moment and to meet what each new moment brings.

- Trust accepts the fact that a genuine relationship is two-sided and therefore beyond the control of our will.

- A corollary of existential trust is existential grace that comes to us from the situation.

- Existential trust cannot be induced by auto-suggestion.

- Existential trust involves the courage to address and the courage to respond.

- The courage to address and the courage to respond include the recognition that there are no formulae as to when and how to address and when and how to respond.

• The courage to respond begins with openness and a willingness to listen to the other. (318–31)

Buber's understanding of trust and turning is drawn largely from his studies in Hasidism and its interpretation of the central terms of Judaism. In the Hasidic tradition the word *turning* emerges from and points back to the biblical term *teshuvah* (turning to God). The Hassidic tradition sees God's glory as dwelling in every living thing. According to Buber, therefore, each human being's role is to bring forth the godliness in all things and to bring about the actualization of God's presence in all actions. Buber uses the Hebrew term *teshuvah* to indicate the action necessary to restore harmony to the world. The Hasidic tales show again and again that meeting can only be a spontaneous action, an appropriate response to the world.

In her book *Buber on God and the Perfect Man* Pamela Vermes highlights the significance of *teshuvah* to Buber's philosophy, stating that each of the words that Buber has written spell this one primary word. The term is so significant as it stands that she stubbornly resists translating it. From her viewpoint, translations such as "conversion" are inevitably misleading. She writes:

> *Teshuvah* is not a return to a sin-free condition. It is a turnabout to face in an opposite direction. It is the beginning of a different journey, not along a way ordered by God, but along a path taken by God's own indwelling Presence. One who makes his *teshuvah* follows in the footsteps of God. (234–35)

Turning How?

The activity of turning, Buber writes in *Pointing the Way,* "involves risk, the risk of giving oneself, of inner transformation" (206).[3] In this context it is helpful to recall briefly the contents page from Buber's little book *The Way of Man: According to the Teaching of Hasidism:*

I. Heart-Searching

II. The Particular Way

III. Resolution

IV. Beginning with Oneself

V. Not to Be Preoccupied with Oneself

VI. Here Where One Stands

It is evident that all these subjects are related and that they follow an order suggestive of a path. The act of "heart-searching" initiates each person's "particular way" or unique task, which is activated by a determined "resolution" to "begin with oneself" and at the same time "not to be preoccupied with oneself." The meaning and significance of heart-searching, this entire course and order of action, begins and culminates "here where one stands." In this inter-dynamic process, the Hasid stands "here where one is" at the intersection of "heart-searching," "particularity," and "resolution."

Thus, by hallowing the everyday, we participate in the process of becoming "humanly holy." In the section titled, "Not to Be Preoccupied with Oneself," Buber pictures turning as almost the greatest of human acts:

> But turning means here something much greater than repentance and acts of penance; it means that by a reversal of his whole being, a man who had been lost in the maze of selfishness where he had always set himself as his goal, finds a way to God, that is, a way to the fulfillment of the particular task for which he, this particular man, has been destined by God. (32)

We have already said that turning is a centered act of shifting focus from ourselves toward others. Rather than self-realization, or self-possession, or self-will, turning involves spontaneous openness to relational events. "In the beginning," as Buber writes, "is relationship." But prior to entering into a genuine relationship, a person needs to completely shift attention toward others, and in the process, toward dialogue itself.

The act of turning, finally, for Buber, is not a mental trick one can master or a technique one can apply, but a movement one makes toward the other. Relying on techniques tends to create a dependency on the method for its own sake, or for the sake of mastering others. Consider the story of an Indian guru who had a certain unconscious way of brushing his teeth. Automatically, he would brush three times on the upper right, three times on the upper left, and then he would gargle and wash his mouth. Next, he proceeded to the lower right and the lower left, and then gargled once again. He then finished with the upper front and then the lower front before a final gargle.

One day he woke up a little earlier than usual and stepped out onto his balcony. There, below in the garden, were several pupils in a line brushing their teeth in unison: first three times on the upper right, and then three times on the upper left before gargling! A technique always includes a specific goal and method, but these soon become instruments of mechanical repetition rather than instruments of human liberation. Unlike any technique, turning involves a willingness to address and respond to the other openly and honestly. According to Buber, turning is the basic movement of one's being. A shift, yes, but not just a shift. The process embodies a fundamental change of basic orientation toward life.

Genuine Listening

One afternoon, after a seminar on Buber's *I and Thou,* a young instructor from the philosophy department (who had been attending the seminar) asked two questions that significantly challenged the context of the seminar: "What does Buber say about how I should enter into relationships? Should I prepare for dialogue in a certain way?" In other words, can one do something before entering dialogue?

We can say that Buber would have answered directly that one cannot prepare for genuine dialogue except by fostering a willingness to relate. But the actual moment of dialogue—its unique particularity—cannot be prepared for. Certainly, then, Buber would also speak of the double act of turning. Turning applies to each soul's will to relationship; by intending to pay full attention, by participating with a spirit of openness, by activating courage and trust, and by being fully present, we can prepare ourselves for the path of dialogue by turning the very foundation of the soul's orientation to the world.

There is, however, a way to begin living dialogically. The life of dialogue requires genuine listening. Indeed, we can say that real listening *initiates* turning. Often, listening is thought of as "active listening," the prescribed encouragement of maximum levels of feedback. "Active listening" is a process that can be practiced.

Genuine listening, for Buber, meant obedient listening. To cultivate dialogue, we are called to become faithfully attentive to the *Thou-person* who speaks, to the words spoken, and just as attentive to the unknowable unique "otherness" of others. Genuine listening, finally, means listening to the very ground on which a person stands. Obedient listening along with real contending comprises the very heart of living dialogue.

ACTIVE LISTENING	OBEDIENT LISTENING
• Having a reason or purpose for listening	• Turning toward the other with one's whole being (body/mind/spirit)
• Suspending judgment	• Being fully present to the uniqueness of the situation with the other
• Resisting distractions	
• Pausing before responding	
• Rephrasing the other's context in one's own words	• Faithfully and attentively responding
• Seeking out the "feelings of the message"	• Imagining what the other is thinking, feeling, perceiving
	• Asking meaning-directed questions
	• Attending both to what is said and to what is not said

Meetings

We have seen that Buber's life concretely exemplifies his philosophy. Indeed, the following anecdote illustrates the main motive of this chapter—turning—by virtue of his early inability to practice it and his subsequent realization of its necessity in life.

The fact that Buber also included this story in his 1929 essay "Dialogue" suggests that it contains a personal statement of elements that appeared in *I and Thou*.

By his mid-thirties Buber had divided his life into moments of ecstasy during which he was lifted out of the ordinary. As World War I was breaking out, in July 1914, a young man came to visit Buber after Buber had experienced a morning of ecstatic reverie. The anecdote that follows is one of the most frequently quoted passages from *Meetings*. It is most often used to reinforce the autobiographical significance of Buber's decisive shift from his earlier mystical stage (a fullness without obligation) to his more mature dialogical stage (willed for a life of communion). The following event was to prove decisive for Buber.

A Conversion

In my earlier years the "religious" was for me the exception. There were hours that were taken out of the course of things. From somewhere or other the firm crust of everyday was pierced. Then the reliable permanence of appearances broke down; the attack which took place burst its law asunder. "Religious experience" was the experience of an otherness which did not fit into the context of life. It could begin with something customary, with consideration of some familiar object, but which then became unexpectedly mysterious and uncanny, finally lighting a way into the lightning-pierced darkness of the mystery itself. But also, without any intermediate stage, time could be torn apart—first the firm world's structure, then the still firmer self-assurance flew apart and you were delivered to fullness. The "religious" lifted you out. Over there now lay the accustomed existence with its affairs, but here illumination and ecstasy and rapture held without time or sequence. Thus your own being encompassed a life here and a life beyond, and there was no bond but the actual moment of the transition.

The illegitimacy of such a division of the temporal life, which is streaming to death and eternity and which only in fulfilling its temporality can be fulfilled in face of these, was brought home to me by an everyday event, an event of judgment, judging with that sentence from closed lips and an unmoved glance such as the ongoing course of things loves to pronounce.

What happened was no more than that one forenoon, after a morning of "religious" enthusiasm, I had a visit from an unknown young man, without being there in spirit. I certainly did not fail to let the meeting be friendly, I did not treat him any more remissly than all his contemporaries who were in the habit of seeking me out about this time of day as an oracle that is ready to listen to reason. I conversed attentively and openly with him—only I omitted to guess the questions which he did not put. Later, not long after, I learned from one of his friends—he himself was no longer alive—the essential content of these questions; I learned that he had come to me not casually, but borne by destiny, not for a chat but for a decision. He had come to me; he had come in this hour. What do we expect when we are in despair and yet go to a man? Surely a presence by means of which we are told that nevertheless there is meaning.

Since then I have given up the "religious" which is nothing but the exception, extraction, exaltation, ecstasy; or it has given me up. I possess nothing but the everyday out of which I am never taken. The mystery is no longer disclosed, it has escaped or it has made its dwelling here where every thing happens where it happens. I know no fullness but each mortal hour's fullness of claim and responsibility. Though far from being equal to it, yet I know that in the claim I am claimed and may respond in responsibility, and know who speaks and demands a response.

I do not know much more. If that is religion then it is just *everything,* simply all that is lived in its possibility of dialogue. Here is space also for religion's highest forms. As when you pray you do not thereby remove yourself from this life of yours but in your praying refer your thought to it, even though it may be in order to yield it; so too in the unprecedented and surprising, when you are called upon from above, required, chosen, empowered, sent, you with this your mortal bit of life are meant. This moment is not extracted from it, it rests on what has been and beckons to the remainder that has still to be lived. You are not swallowed up in a fullness without obligation, you are willed for the life of communion. (45–46)

While the young student and Buber in this story conversed attentively, Buber failed to turn to him completely. In other words, he failed to grasp fundamental life questions that the student did not ask directly. That is, Buber failed to hear or notice the young man's deeper concerns that remained beneath the surface of speech. Buber had not been fully attentive, fully present. Nor had he listened obediently.

In his 1957 dialogue with Carl Rogers, Buber, referring to this episode, spoke of persons for whom the world has become baseless, those who have lost their ground. They do not seek only for another person to trust them but seek an "existential trust." Reflecting on this story, Maurice Friedman writes in *Intercultural Dialogue and the Human Image*:

> The existential guilt that Buber felt was not that he did not remove the young man's despair, but that he was not present as a whole person. Therefore, he did not bring the resources that he might have had to that meeting. (53)

Buber wrote in a letter to Friedman that the young man was killed at the front in World War I out of a "despair which did not oppose his own death." Friedman writes in *Meetings:*

> The young man...did not look to Buber as the magic helper who would reach into his soul and extract his question. He did not simply *have* a question: he concentrated his whole being into *becoming* a question. It was the address of this unspeakable question that Buber might have heard behind every question that Herr Mehé *did* ask if Martin Buber had been "present in spirit"—if he had brought himself into the dialogue with the whole of his being, rather than with the intellectual and social fragments left over from his preoccupation with his morning of mystic ecstasy. (10–11)

On mornings wrapped in "religious enthusiasm," genuine meeting could not occur. Had Buber fully opened himself to the address of the young man—presence-to-presence in the moment of meeting—the despair beneath the man's words could have been disclosed. Buber thought of this grave mismeeting not only as a judgment on his whole way of life but also as providing the unified, event-centered elements that later would appear as principles of genuine dialogue.

Practice Exercises

1. What do I bring to my relationship to an individual *Thou?*

2. Think about an event in your life in which withholding your stand created a conflict. Describe the conflict and suggest how you might have avoided it. Next, think about an event in your life in which the stand you took enriched the relationship and generated genuine dialogue. Describe it. Compare these events.

3. Have you ever had a conversion experience? If so, describe its details. What were you like before? What were you like afterward? If not, reflect on what it is that would most prevent such an experience from occurring in your life. Share your responses with a partner. Is genuine dialogue present in the midst of your reflections?

4. Arrange yourselves in conversational pairs, facing each other. Take turns speaking and listening to each other about a subject in this chapter that has significance for your life. Take turns repeating back to your partner what you heard your partner say. Discuss what you learned from this process.

5. Reflect on Buber's conversion story. From what did he convert? What caused it? Do you see yourself in his story? If so, where? If not, why? Can you imagine yourself giving up either religious experience (if you are religious) or peak experience (if you are not)?

6. In what sense does the act of turning involve personal trust? Can personal trust be learned? Can it be practiced? To what extent can one induce and/or stimulate personal trust? Imagine yourself in a situation in which you are

fully trusting. Describe the situation. What is the most difficult obstacle for you to overcome in this situation?

Notes

1. Kaufmann's translation is better than Smith's because he keeps the Buberian sentence structure and thus makes it clearer that Buber is referring to the anxiety people feel when entering relationships. Buber uses the term *Selbsterhaltungstrieb,* which Smith translates with "self-asserting instinct" and Kaufmann with "self-affirmation." Kaufmann's translation here is much closer to the content of the German text.

2. Buber uses the word *Reich,* which Smith translates with "Kingdom." Kaufmann translates with "realm." Although *Reich* can mean, in certain contexts, "kingdom," in this context Buber means "realm."

3. In *Pointing the Way* Buber writes: "Inner transformation simply means surpassing one's present factual constitution; it means that the person one is intended to be penetrates what has appeared up till now, that the customary soul enlarges and transfigures itself into the surprise soul" (206).

Postscript

Frequently Asked Questions

Again and again readers have asked me what I might have meant here or there. For a long time I answered each individually, but gradually I saw that I could not do justice to these demands, and moreover I surely must not restrict the dialogical relationship to those readers who decide to speak up: perhaps some of those who remain silent deserve special consideration. Hence I resolved to answer publicly—first of all a few essential questions that are interrelated.

—Martin Buber (Kaufmann, 171)

Chapter 7

The Way of "Inclusion"

*Man must practice the kind of realization
which I call inclusion.*

In the 1923 edition of *I and Thou,* the last page of the text simply reads: "Conception of the work whose beginning is represented by this book: spring 1916; first complete draft of this book: fall 1919; final version: spring 1922." In the 1958 edition, these lines were omitted and replaced by the "Postscript."

Buber's "Postscript," intended to clarify and expand his discussion of the treasured dialogical relationships "hidden in our midst," was written in Jerusalem during October 1957 and was included in the second addition of *I and Thou.* The "Postscript" *(Nachwort)* both stands apart from *I and Thou* (separated from the first edition by almost forty years) and remains vitally connected to his classic text and to Buber's philosophical development. It stands as one of Buber's responses to frequently asked questions from students and colleagues about the meaning of his thought. It also contains several new and significant developments in his thinking.

For one thing, the "Postscript" adds a relational realm of *I-Thou* mutuality and calls attention both to distinctions between and within them and to the "unity and wholeness" beneath them. Indeed, one of his most important additions in the "Postscript" is a discussion of a fourth relational realm. To *I-Thou* relationships with nature, with spirit becoming forms, and with persons, he added *I-Thou* relationships with the "eternal *Thou*." While we discussed this earlier (Chapters 2 and 5), it is important here to remember that Buber added the fourth relational realm almost four decades after finishing his book. In addition, Buber used the "Postscript" to introduce his understanding of what he calls the "normative limitation of mutuality." And, most significant, he introduces the image of God as "absolute Person" who is always entering into relationships with persons.

Suprapersonal Vision

In the opening paragraph of the "Postscript" Buber reveals his motivation for writing *I and Thou,* which suggests that this question must have come up again and again in his public life. He tells us that he was impelled by an inward necessity, by a vision that had repeatedly come to him since his youth; that he wished to clarify publicly particular meanings; and that this clarity was manifestly suprapersonal in its nature. He begins:

SMITH, 123
INWARD NECESSITY

When I drafted the first sketch of this book (more than forty years ago), I was impelled by an inward necessity. A vision which had come to me again and again since my youth, and which had been clouded again and again, had now reached steady clarity. This clarity was so manifestly suprapersonal in its nature that I at once knew I had to bear witness to it.

KAUFMANN, 169
INNER NECESSITY

When I drafted the first sketch of this book (more than forty years ago), I felt impelled by an inner necessity. A vision that had afflicted me repeatedly since my youth but had always been dimmed again, had now achieved a constant clarity that was so evidently suprapersonal that I soon knew that I ought to bear witness to it.

Buber's vision, of course, is not a mystically heightened inner experience but (according to his 1929 essay "Dialogue," published in *Between Man and Man*) an image of the human. In one sentence Buber enunciates in "Dialogue" what he calls in *I and Thou* his "most essential concern"—"the close connexion of the relation to God with the relation to one's fellow-man" (123–24). Kaufmann's word "association" more accurately translates the German *Verbundenheit:* an unconditional, mutual embracing and inclusive reciprocity of deep bonding.

Five Questions

At this point Buber quickly states his primary reason for writing the "Postscript." "Again and again," he remarks, "readers have turned to me to ask about the meaning of this and that" (Smith, 124). While gladly responding to these questions as often as possible in life, he claims that he came to realize at some point the impossibility of answering everyone:

SMITH, 124 PUBLIC ANSWER	KAUFMANN, 171 ANSWER PUBLICLY
For a long time I answered each individually, but I gradually realised that I was not able to do justice to the demand laid upon me; besides, I must not limit the dialogical relationship to those readers who make up their minds to speak: perhaps there are many among the silent who deserve special consideration. So I have had to set about giving a public answer, first of all to some essential questions which are bound together by their meaning.	For a long time I answered each individually, but gradually I saw that I could not do justice to these demands, and moreover I surely must not restrict the dialogical relationship to those readers who decide to speak up: perhaps some of those who remain silent deserve special consideration. Hence I resolved to answer publicly— first of all a few essential questions that are interrelated.

To help himself focus on those questions that seemed most important, early in 1957, as he was preparing for a new German edition of *I and Thou*, Buber asked Maurice Friedman to provide him with a list of questions that Friedman felt most often occurred to readers of the book. In the following pages we attempt to provide a brief yet thorough outline of the structure of the "Postscript" (from Smith's version) by focusing on the questions that Buber chose to address. Of the questions gathered by Friedman, Buber selected five, which are bound together by the theme of mutuality. As an overview of the "Postscript," then, it seems reasonable to begin with a straight-forward list of these questions and Buber's basic answers to them.

First, if the I-Thou *relationship requires mutuality that embraces both* I *and* Thou, *what is the character of this reciprocity in our relationship with nature?*

Buber distinguishes between different realms of nature: (1) the liminal realm on the threshold of language in our relations with animals, and (2) the preliminal, nonverbal relations we have with plants. Relationships with animals share with human relationships the quality of spontaneity and thus have a latent mutuality. Relationships with plants do not include mutual spontaneity, and therefore the reciprocity of "being in its course" (126) discloses itself to the "sayer of *Thou*" (126) as unity and wholeness. Relationships with stones and stars are also preliminal.

Second, concerning the supraliminal sphere, above the threshold of language, the sphere of spirit, where is mutuality to be found?

Buber elucidates another twofold distinction to answer the question of how we relate to spirits or the spiritual realm. We relate to the spiritual through (1) the "structures of spirit" (127) that have already entered the world, and (2) the spirit that has not yet entered the world but is ready to do so. The writings and sayings of dead masters offer one example of spirits already in the world, living through the text and word. A relatively static art form like a Doric pillar is a spirit waiting to enter the world. In each example a person is required to call the spirit forth by saying *Thou* to the form it takes. Without this saying of *Thou*, the spirit, whether in or outside the world, does not manifest.

> ***Third, reconsidering the relationship with nature and spirit, can we speak of a "response" or "address" that comes from an order of being lacking spontaneity or consciousness? Is nature such an order of being?***

Both in the realm of nature and in the realm of spirit, the spirit that lives on in word and in work, and the spirit that wishes to become word and work affects us by its "ongoing course of being" or its presentness of being (p. 131).

> ***Fourth, concerning mutuality itself as the door into our existence, is the* I-Thou *relationship between humans always entirely reciprocal?***

Quite simply, no. There are two limitations to reciprocal mutuality: (1) human insufficiency (estrangement, melancholy), and (2) the inner laws that govern our life together. Some *I-Thou* relationships, by their very nature, never unfold into complete mutuality.

A few examples of dialogues that are not mutual are the dialogues between students and teachers, therapists and clients, pastors and parishioners. The teaching and healing and ministering relationships would become different kinds of relationships altogether if the student, patient, or parishioner were called to imagine the other's side. They would become friendships, and the patient, for example, would become concerned with the doctor's health. Needless to say, there is a social limitation on how far dialogue can become mutual in contexts like these. Buber called this limitation the "normative limitation of mutuality" (132).

> ***Fifth, how can our relationship to the eternal* Thou *be exclusive and yet include all other* I-Thou *relationships?***

An answer to this question is only possible if we describe God not as a principle, an idea, or an abstract being, but as a Person in relationship with us. Described this way, God enters direct relationship with us as an "eternal *Thou*" in this world. In either case—whether in "Person" or through a person—God speaks to us in all *I-Thou* dialogues. The speech of the "absolute Person" transforms life events into "instruction, message, [and] demand" (136).

The Four Realms Revisited

Each of these questions, in one way or another, addresses the issue of reciprocity between dialogical partners: its possibility, its fullness, and its limitations. Buber's addition of the fourth relational realm serves, in part, to account for the eternal possibility of inclusion. Because the "eternal *Thou*" cannot become an "*It*," the "*Thou*" is always accessible to us. A person relates to God as "the alone to the Alone" (*Philosophical Interrogations,* 85). Just so, we come out of our isolation to address one another.

Even though the "eternal *Thou*" is glimpsed throughout *I and Thou,* only in the "Postscript" does Buber speak of our dialogue with God.

"Postscript" Relational Realms

Nature beneath language	Liminal (Threshold) with animals	Preliminal with plants/trees
Spirit Becoming Forms begets language	Supraliminal spirit prior to form	Spirit manifested in forms
Humans uses language	Inclusion	Normative limitation of mutuality
Eternal *Thou* penetrates language	Beyond knowing	**Absolute Person**

The four relational realms move from meeting that which is "beneath language," to that which "begets language" (art, knowledge, action), to the one who "uses language," to the One who "penetrates language." The sequential logic of this relational arrangement sets up couplets of relatedness: "nature" and "spirit becoming forms" are paired (without language) as are "humans" and the "eternal *Thou*" (using language). With language, without language: each pair is formed by its unique connection or closeness to speech.

Since our relation with nature is beneath speech, our risk of being wounded by relationships at this level is not substantial. And since our relationship with spirit becoming forms begets speech, the same holds true. However, when we enter into relationship with a human *Thou*, we open ourselves to the possibility that our partner will stop talking or speak hurtfully. The possibility of becoming wounded when relationships enter the level of language is substantially greater.

Of course, the same does not hold for the "eternal *Thou*." Here, there is no risk of being wounded. Or rather, the only risk comes from our side of the relationship, where we experience the pain of self-inflicted isolation from unconditional love. It is ultimately this sense of isolation that makes reciprocity possible—and the "eternal *Thou*" is its eternal reminder. Because we know the experience of being alone, we naturally long to be in dialogue. The presence of "eternal *Thou*," an unseen company we keep, calls us into the world of relational speech.

Boldly Swinging

Inclusion, experiencing the other's side in a relationship, is at the core of human interactions. The act of inclusion occurs when one imagines what the other is feeling, thinking, and experiencing without giving up the felt reality of one's own activity. This activity is almost contradictory. While we must necessarily hold our ground of subjectivity to be human, we also feel called to go out and meet an other. Thus we live in a kind of tension, or narrow ridge, between the *I* and the *Thou*.

Maurice Friedman, in his study *Religion and Psychology: A Dialogical Approach*, coined the metaphor of "a bold imaginative swinging" to describe how we overcome this dialectical razor. "This means seeing through the eyes of the other and experiencing the other's side of the relationship *without* ceasing to experience the relationship from one's own side" (38). "Boldly swinging" refers here to the combination of a willing imagination, a temporary suspension of one-sided speech, and thinking/willing/experiencing on both sides of the relationship in a common situation.

The capacity to swing boldly involves two nearly simultaneous movements: (1) swinging *over* to the other's side, and (2) then bringing *back* to my own side as much of the other's situation as I can glean not as detached content but as a living process. Though I cannot become another person, I can go as far as possible to experience the relationship from the other person's perspective. In response to a comment that inclusion must be difficult, Friedman reports that Buber once responded: "It's not difficult at all, it's a grace."[1]

This process is made all the more important because my responses are influenced in turn by perspectives I have brought back from the experience of swinging to the other's side. Buber calls this capacity inclusion.

Inclusion

Inclusion comprises several facets:

1. Meaning the other; experiencing the other's side in relationship;

2. Living the other's part in a common situation;

3. Being willing to stand again and again at both poles of relationship; and

4. Experiencing the effect of reciprocal interaction.

In this relational practice I discover that I am living the other's part in a common situation and can speak directly to the heart of it. I become intimately part of another's "meaning," and by "meaning the other" I stand on both poles of our knowing together. I do not just experience the other's pains and sorrows, but when the relationship is mutual, I begin experiencing the effect of reciprocal interaction.

"Experiencing the other's side" embodies, for Buber, feeling two sides at once. The greater a person's inclusiveness, the more a person is able to be present in his or her own actuality. The more inclusive a person becomes, the more that person becomes included in his or her own life. Yet inclusion is not empathy. *Empathy*, for Buber, meant going to the other's side while giving up one's position. By going over to the other side, when I completely empathize with the other, I lose myself. Or conversely, seeing only my self in the other, I lose the interhuman ground on which I stand and dialogue becomes impossible. "Inclusion," on the other hand, means that one is present at one's own side as well as on the other's side. This two-sided presence is the most intense stirring of one's being—concretely imagining what the other is experiencing, not as the content of thought, but as the ongoing process of human becoming.

But because we've put so much emphasis on inclusion, it seems reasonable to return to the question, Is dialogue always two-sided?

The Buber-Rogers Dialogue

In April 1957, shortly before writing his "Postscript," a dialogue was arranged between Buber and the noted American psychologist Carl Rogers, founder of the client-centered or nondirective approach to psychotherapy. Buber was seventy-nine at the time. Rogers was fifty-five. The hour-and-a-half conversation was conducted on stage before an audience of four hundred people at the University of Michigan. Because it explicitly focused on the nature of dialogue, the Buber-Rogers dialogue represents a rich resource for understanding *I and Thou*. The dialogue was moderated by Maurice Friedman and appears at the end of Buber's *The Knowledge of Man*.

Rogers's opening question tellingly compliments Buber while clearly privileging the psychotherapist's profession: "How have you lived so deeply in interpersonal relationships and gained such an understanding of the human individual," he asked, "without being a psychotherapist?" (167). Buber responded autobiographically, speaking of his study of psychology and about what was most important to him—namely, his inclination to meet fully each person, to establish a *real* relationship, and to remain open to change.

A few moments later in the dialogue, Rogers raised the possibility that Buber's "genuine dialogue" might be similar to what he, Rogers, called "effective moments in the therapeutic relationship." In the course of their conversation Buber had expressed concern with the limits of genuine dialogue in some situations, and the question of whether all dialogical relationships are inclusive seemed ready to hatch. Are there not some relationships that must remain one-sided? Buber explained to Rogers that psychotherapeutic dialogues are not reciprocal at all because of the "normative limitation of mutuality" we spoke of earlier.

This response led to a pressing discussion between them. Rogers insisted that in moments "when another person is really expressing himself and his experience...I don't feel [as a therapist], in the way that you've described, different from him" (172). Rogers maintained that complete mutuality existed between himself and his clients. According to Rogers, in the therapeutic situation there can be "a meeting of two persons on an equal basis—even though, in the world of I-It, it could be seen as a very unequal relationship" (173).

At this point Buber disagreed, expressing concern with the "objective" therapist-client *situation* as a species entirely distinct from Rogers's experience of it. Full mutuality, Buber held, does not exist between a therapist and a client as long as that relationship continues to occur in the context of therapy. Admitting that he was not a therapist, Buber climactically announced, "I must see you and him in this [unequal] dialogue bounded by tragedy" (174). The possibility of a healing relationship would be terminated the moment that tragedy ended and the patient was able to experience the psychotherapist's side of the relationship.

In the "Postscript" to *I and Thou,* giving some consideration to his meeting with Rogers, Buber reiterated that "full mutuality is not inherent in man's life together" (Smith, 131). It is here that Buber introduces the term "normative limitation of mutuality" that he applied to dialogues in helping relationships and helping professions. Therapeutic situations include a mutuality of contact and of cooperation existing on both sides, a mutuality of concern for a common problem, but the responsibility and concern for the other lies primarily on the therapist's side. The patient is responsible only for expressing his problem.

One-Sided Inclusion

Relationships of full mutuality (like deep friendships in which inclusion is two-sided) are the most fulfilling expressions of dialogical relationships. But often, mutual inclusion and mutual concern are not possible or even desirable. In Buber's three examples of necessarily one-sided relationships—those involving pastors, teachers, and therapists—"the between" becomes a kind of one-sided event.

In the teaching dialogue, for example, the teacher experiences the student's side of the relationship, but the opposite is rarely possible, unless the student experiences the teacher's learning. When the student experiences the world from the teacher's side, the nature of the educational relationship shifts, and teacher and student become friends. Or perhaps they become colleagues, in which case their concerns are decidedly mutual. To put it another way, while the teacher experiences that a student is being educated, the student does not normally experience the education of the teacher. Advanced students do show interest, and better teachers do acknowledge their position as learners in the world, but students in these classrooms still normally experience their teachers as those with the ability to pass on their knowledge.

By stating that a teaching relationship is necessarily one-sided, Buber does not mean that a teacher relates to a student as an *It*. The one-sided inclusion of teaching can become an *I-Thou* relationship when it is grounded in a common situation, in mutuality and trust. Full mutuality, though, is "a great gift." Indeed, "it is a grace, for which one must always be ready and which one never gains as an assured possession" (Smith, 131).

SMITH, 132 INCLUSION	KAUFMANN, 178 EMBRACING
And in order that his effect upon him may be a unified and significant one he must also live this situation, again and again, in all its moments not merely from his own end but also from that of his partner: he must practise the kind of realisation which I call inclusion *(Umfassung)*.	And to give his influence unity and meaning, he must live through this situation in all its aspects not only from his own point of view but also from that of his partner. He must practice the kind of realization that I call embracing. It is essential that he should awaken the I-You relationship in the pupil, too, who should intend and affirm his educator as this particular person; and yet the educational relationship could not endure if the pupil also practiced the art of embracing by living through the shared situation from the educator's point of view. Whether the I-You relationship comes to an end or assumes the altogether different character of a friendship, it becomes clear that the specifically educational relationship is incompatible with complete mutuality.
But however much depends upon his awakening the *I-Thou* relationship in the pupil as well—and however much depends upon the pupil, too, meaning and affirming him as the particular person he is—the special educative relation could not persist if the pupil for his part practised "inclusion," that is, if he lived the teacher's part in the common situation. Whether the *I-Thou* relationship now comes to an end or assumes the quite different character of a friendship, it is plain that the specifically educative relation as such is denied full mutuality.	

Here, Smith's translation of the German *Umfassung* is preferable to Kaufmann's "embracing," which would be a better translation for the word *Verbundenheit*. In Smith's version, though, when the pupil "lived the teacher's part in the common situation," we are left with the suggestion of a common identity between students and teachers. Kaufmann preserves Buber's emphasis on the two-sided nature of normative classroom events: one practices "the art of embracing [inclusion] by living through the *shared* [not common] situation" from the other's viewpoint (italics added).

Making Present

Mishael Caspi, professor in the Department of Philosophy and Religious Studies at Bates College, Maine, exemplifies what has been said about the constituents of "inclusion" in his personal account of meeting Buber for the first time:

> My earliest memory of Professor Martin Buber was at a seminar he gave in the teacher training college which he created in the fifties in Israel. I remember in a class of about seven or eight, he talked about the book of Genesis and the creation of the world. With his smiling eyes and white beard, he talked in a way that bewildered me. Sometimes, I felt what he was saying was much beyond me.
>
> At one point, he said something about his concept of creation which I did not fully understand. I raised my hand and he stopped talking and asked me what I wanted to say. "I would very much like to know what is your conception of the creation of the world." And try to understand, while I was raised in a very orthodox house, I had just finished my service in the army. Being a member of the Kibutz, I was between Orthodoxy and a denial of all its teaching. So I really wanted to understand how other people view the creation.
>
> In a very beautiful Jewish way he said to me: "What is creation for you?" I looked at him with surprise at the fact that he wanted to know from me what I wanted to know from him. I stuttered at first, and then I said: "I think that creation is to be a part of what is happening, a part of creation." And he shook his head and said, "No, no, no! It is to be together *with* creation." It took me a long time to be able to understand the difference between "to be a part *of*" and "to be a part *with*." In many senses I understood later on that Buber's

response emphasized for me the whole concept of *I and Thou* in a very simple way.

By crossing over to his side of their meeting, by concretely imagining what he was thinking and feeling, Buber gained insight into the situation of Mishael's question that, in turn, led him to question the questioner and cut to the heart of the matter. Buber's practice of "inclusion" allowed him to provide an answer that would continue to flower in Mishael's understanding and open for him the fruitfulness of a basic *I-Thou* address.

The impact of Buber's response merely underscored his question. In many ways Buber's practice of inclusion was his answer to the question of Adam. To answer God's question "Where are you," we might reply, "Here on the ground of inclusion"—on the ground where genuine dialogue, turning, and imagining the real all bring the senses together with one's perceptions of the other.

But how does this happen? Buber maintains that imagining the real, finally, is not a subjective activity. It does not just arise from one's own efforts. Instead, it arises as the result of mutual concern between human beings. Really seeing the other is finally possible only when there is some form of relational reciprocity and equality. And this is possible to the extent that I am willing to pass beyond subjective experiencing in order to make the other present as he or she alone.[2]

Dialogical relationships, therefore, reach their highest perfection in this making present, grounded in a capacity for imagining the real, holding before one's soul a reality arising in the moment that cannot be personally contained. Making present means that I imagine to myself personally what another person is, at this very moment, wishing, feeling, perceiving, and thinking.

Making the Other Present

How do we make the other present? Buber pointed out these steps:

1. Practicing inclusion while maintaining your stand.

2. Realizing the other person's actual uniqueness.

3. Realizing the other person's potential wholeness.

4. Viewing the other person as fully meaningful.

Landauer's Death

"Personally making present" is a living process of seeing the whole person. It calls for practicing inclusion while maintaining a personal ground, viewing the other as individually meaningful, and realizing the other's potential wholeness. A powerful illustration of what Buber means by "making the other present" is exemplified in Friedman's retelling of the way Buber received news of Gustav Landauer's death. Next to his relationship with Paula, his friendship with Gustav Landauer was one of the defining relationships of his life. Landauer, a pacifist socialist dedicated to Judaically infused humanitarian idealism and social reform, embodied, for Buber, the personal responsibility of the revolutionary spirit.

In a May 12, 1916, letter to Buber, Landauer wrote:

> You deny precisely that which is most essential through the employment of your vacuous method: you contemplate the everyday and declare it a wonder; you do not encounter the everyday with a formative vision; rather, you attempt to dovetail it into your schemata.

According to Paul Mendez-Flohr in his study *From Mysticism to Dialogue,* Landauer's letter "was of major significance in Buber's personal and intellectual biography." This letter contains a "pivotal factor (among others), in Buber's turn from mysticism...to the philosophy of dialogue" (102). Landauer's pacifist resistance to the war (in the days of postwar chaos) was even more radical than Buber's own.

Buber was devastated by the news of Landauer's death. Soldiers of the Third Reich had beaten, kicked, and finally shot Landauer to death in the Stadelheim prison where he had been taken for questioning. As Maurice Friedman writes in *Encounter on the Narrow Ridge:*

> Buber's response to the news of Landauer's death was proba-
> bly, next to his "conversion" and the early separation from
> his mother, the most important single event in his life. Yet this
> is one "autobiographical fragment" that Buber could not
> write. When I urged him to do so in Jerusalem in 1960, he
> confessed he had tried and found himself still too close to this
> event to be able to write about it. (114)

On receiving news of Landauer's barbaric murder, Buber reported that he "was compelled to imagine this killing, not only visually, but with my *body*" (115).

The Spirit of Dialogue

Making the other person present, according to Buber, depends on one's ability to *accept* and *affirm* and *confirm* the other as a uniquely whole, present being. Of the three behaviors, confirmation is most important. In *The Knowledge of Man* Buber writes that the basis of interpersonal life is the wish of each person to be confirmed as what that person actually is, even as what he or she can become. Rinzai Zen Buddhist philosopher Nishitani Keiji remarks:

> Dialogue begins not from an undisputed object of faith, not
> from any central dogma, or "I," but from a letting go of the
> ego and a submission to reasonableness....Its spirit is the
> spirit of inquiry and discovery.[3]

For Buber, the spirit of dialogue embodies both letting go of reflexive tendencies and submitting to the presence of mutuality.

In this spirit, confirming another person involves both (1) acceptance of a person in the moment, and (2) acceptance of the person's potential. It could be said that if love is to flourish, the act of confirmation between people is necessary. Confirmation is a deeply held human yearning to be accepted and affirmed in one's uniqueness despite disagreements. Confirmation arises out of endless sources and contexts (social, familial, and vocational, just to start with).[4] Wherever there is an ability to share suffering and pain, it calls forth the other's deepest expressions.

Mutual confirmation, accordingly, is most fully realized in the act of "making present." And making the other present is generated by the capacity to "imagine the real." By making the other present, we confirm the inmost self-becoming of our partners in dialogue. In this perspective Buber distinguished among three interrelated pointings or orientations in this kind of genuine dialogue: *acceptance, affirmation,* and *confirmation.* These interlinked behaviors move from generic acceptance (accepting the other as a person like myself), to specific affirmation (affirming the other in his or her unique historic, cultural, or ethnic personhood, and so on), to confirming the other (validating the other's present stance and his or her direction of movement into the future).

Confirming another is a complex interaction because it includes co-participation between persons in here-and-now situations and also extends the promise to participate in future dialogue. Confirmation includes mutual contact, mutual trust, and mutual concern for all the issues being discussed; that is, I confirm you as you are in the present moment and as who you will become in the future (without necessarily agreeing with you). Confirming you as you will be and accepting that you will change, I open a path to the future of *I* and *Thou.*

Confirmation, furthermore, adds to acceptance and affirmation the willingness to continue challenging the other to move in the direction his or her life is taking. I affirm the other's will, as well as his or her identity. Since these three interactions are intrinsic for implementing an effective practice of inclusion, it is essential to grasp their interconnections. These interlinked behaviors move from accepting the other as a person like myself, to specifically affirming the other in their unique historic, cultural, or ethnic personhood, to validating the other's present stance and their direction of movement into the future.

Bearing Witness

Buber concludes his "Postscript," and thereby concludes the 1958 edition of *I and Thou*, by describing mutuality in the fourth realm, between God and humans. Mutuality, as Buber notes, cannot be proven any more than the existence of God can be proven. Both are borne out only by practical experience in the varieties of genuine dialogue.

SMITH, 137 BEARS WITNESS	KAUFMANN, 182 BEARS WITNESS
The existence of mutuality between God and man cannot be proved, just as God's existence cannot be proved. Yet he dares to speak of it, bears witness, and calls to witness him to whom he speaks—whether that witness is now or in the future.	The existence of mutuality between God and man cannot be proved anymore than the existence of God. Anyone who dares nevertheless to speak of it bears witness and invokes the witness of those whom he addresses—present or future witness.

Finally, practicing genuine dialogue embodies what Buber calls "bearing witness" to the invaluable jewel of an authentic relationship. At the end of *Pointing the Way*, Buber responds to a significant barrier to authentic dialogue, the underlying "pathology of our time," the ever-present danger and fear of losing trust in our capacities for unreserved relationship:[5]

> I believe, despite all, that the peoples in this hour can enter into dialogue, into a genuine dialogue with one another. In a genuine dialogue each of the partners, even when he stands in opposition to the other, heeds, affirms, and confirms his opponent as an existing other. (238)

Meetings

We conclude with a passage from the Introduction to Buber's book *Daniel*. Here, Buber tells of an incident in which the significance of inclusion became a reality to him.

The Walking Stick and the Tree

After a descent during which I had to utilize without a halt the late light of a dying day, I stood on the edge of a meadow, not sure of the safe way, and let the twilight come down upon me. Not needing a support and yet willing to accord my lingering a fixed point, I pressed my stick against a trunk of an oak tree. Then I felt in twofold fashion my contact with being: here, where I held the stick, and there, where I touched the bark. Appearing to be only where I was, I nonetheless found myself there, too, where I found the tree.

At that time dialogue appeared to me. For the speech of man, wherever it is genuine speech, is like that stick; that means: truly directed address. Here, where I am, where ganglia and organs of speech help me to form and to send forth the word, here I "mean" him to whom I send it, I intend him, this one unexchangeable man. But also there, where he is, something of me is delegated, something that is not at all substantial in nature like that being-here, rather pure vibration and incomprehensible; that remains there, with him, the man meant by me, and takes part in the receiving of my word. I encompass [include] him to whom I turn. (47)

Notice that by touching the oak tree with his stick, Buber feels his contact with the tree in a "twofold fashion." He becomes aware of being both here *and* there. Like the stick, the "truly directed address" of human speech connects the unique wholeness of one to that of another. The penultimate sentence is doubly striking. When we leave behind the non-substantial, incomprehensible "pure vibration" of mystical connection, what remains there with the other "takes part in the receiving of my word." Without self-absorption, we become able to offer ourselves up for the meeting. Affirming the other means offering the self in this way.

Practice Exercises

1. If I choose to live dialogue, how do I practice inclusion when I address a *Thou?*

2. Imagine, as concretely as you can, Buber's pressing his walking stick against the bark of the oak tree. Describe an example in your life of feeling a similar twofold sensation. What was it like on your side? What was it like on the other side? When Buber says—"The speech of man, wherever it is genuine speech, is like that stick"—what do you think he means?

3. Write your own "Postscript" in several short statements. In other words, if you were Buber, having written *I and Thou,* what would you choose to add or clarify? What questions would you try to answer? How might you answer them?

4. In *Philosophical Interrogations* Buber wrote: "The great trust, as for example it is expressed with unconditional clarity in Psalm 73, is a *personal* trust of the person as such; it was and is for me the decisive one, except that it has grown and ever again grows on the ground of that experience and hope of Israel" (109). What is the great unbroken trust of your life? What is the great broken trust? How do the effects of these two types of trust enter your relationships? How is it possible to go from a distrustful to a trustful stand in the world after the experience of trust broken?

5. In a conversation about some aspect of this chapter, attempt to imagine with a partner what the other person is thinking, experiencing, and feeling. Then, discuss what you think you understood about your partner. Try, for example, to describe the details of your meeting from the other's point of view. How does your perspective of the other differ from his or her self-perception? Ask, find out, and discuss this question.

6. One way of understanding *I and Thou* arises by comparing what Buber wrote in his original edition to what he wrote in his "Postscript." If the original edition is one partner in a dialogue and the "Postscript" the other partner, what might they say to each other? Do they agree completely? How are they similar? How are they different? What difference does the difference make?

Notes

1. In "A Conversation with Maurice Friedman," with Jeanie Czubaroff, *Southern Communication Journal* 65 (Winter/Spring 2000), 251.

2. In the section "Personal Making Present" in *The Knowledge of Man,* Buber writes: "To be aware of a man, therefore, means in particular to perceive his wholeness as a person determined by the spirit; it means to perceive the dynamic center which stamps his every utterance, action, and attitude with the recognizable sign of uniqueness" (78–80).

3. Nishitani Keiji, *Nishida Kitaro* (Berkeley and Los Angeles: University of California Press, 1991), 43.

4. So important was confirmation for Buber that Maurice Friedman once taught a course entitled "Religion and Psychotherapy" at Temple University in which the main theme was the issue of confirmation and its relationship to the philosophy of genuine dialogue.

5. In *Martin Buber and the Theater,* Maurice Friedman writes: "Buber's mystery-play *Elijah* contains in dramatic form all [the] central motifs in Buber's understanding of biblical and Jewish existence: the demand that the covenant with Israel places on the people...; the task of building the covenant of peace with other nations and of building true community; [and the task of remaining] faithful to the covenant to set the dialogue right through free and wholehearted response" (106).

Glossary of
Buber's Key Terms

Between. *Zwischen* refers to the immediate presence of unreserved, spontaneous mutuality common to each person, yet beyond the sphere of either. Impossible to objectify, "the between" is the most real reality of human existence, of being wholly and uniquely "human" with humans.

Community. *Gemeinschaft* refers to a vital intersection between persons standing toward a living center as well as toward each other in ever-renewed reciprocal giving and receiving.

Confirmation. *Bestätigung* is the act of continuing to take a stand in the presence of the other, affirming, accepting, and supporting the other in his or her uniqueness, and opposing the other when necessary.

Deep Bonding. *Verbundenheit* (translated by Smith and Kaufmann as "connexion") comes from the German verb *verbinden*, which plays with the image of wrapping a gauze around something. *Verbundenheit*, therefore, reflects a deep bonding between dialogical partners.

Dialogue. *Gespräch* happens in open, direct, mutual, present communication (spoken or silent) between persons who speak spontaneously without withholding or promoting an agenda.

Eternal *Thou*. *Das ewige Du* refers to the beginingless and endless *Thou* that can never become an *It*, never an object of our experience; nor can it be used. The "eternal *Thou*" happens by grace and can be glimpsed in genuine relationships.

Experience. *Erfahrung* refers to perceiving the phenomenal world through sensations and concepts in order to use, analyze, or classify.

Experience, Lived. *Erlebnis* refers to deeper experience, to affective, immediate realization of the noumenal or nonrational world grasped in its own splendor.

Grace. *Gnade* refers to the spirit of "the between" that arises from, generates, and supports genuine, interhuman meetings.

Inborn *Thou*. *Das eingeborene Du* refers to the human proclivity toward relationship called forth by the parent who responds to the child's reaching out. Buber calls it our "human birthright."

Inclusion. *Umfassung* refers to "making present," to an act of imagining what the other person is thinking, feeling, and experiencing (not as detached content but as a living process) without surrendering one's own stand.

Individual. *Eigenwesen* refers to self-existing individuals who put their needs into the center of their actions and stand to the world in an *I-It* relation.

Interhuman. *Das Zwischenmenschliche* refers to the interactive region between persons in a genuine relationship. The "interhuman" is the spirit of "the between" through which a person can glimpse the "eternal *Thou*."

Man. *Mensch* refers to a human being (male or female) who embodies and expresses full humanness.

Meeting. *Begegnung* refers to an engaging interaction or direct communication between our innermost being and who/what presents itself to us. The word *Begegnung* only signifies the actual occurrence of engaging and being engaged.

Mutuality. *Gegenseitigkeit* refers to the full, spontaneous, and reciprocal participation of each partner in genuine relationship.

Person. *Person* refers to one who wholly enters into relationship with a *Thou,* accepting the other as an equal partner while yet taking a personal stand. Buber consistently maintains a contrast between *person* and *individual (Eigenwesen).*

Present/Presence. *Gegenwart* can mean either "present" or "presence." Therefore, "presence" has a double dynamic: (1) being fully "there" without withholding oneself; and (2) being fully "open" to enter into ever-renewed dialogue with others.

Primary Words. *Grundworte* (literally translated as "ground words") refers to words that, when spoken, constitute primary life stands—*I-Thou* and *I-It*—which are most fundamental and most meaningful.

Redemption. *Erlösung* refers to God's unconditionally reaching out to humans through relationships, liberating those who respond with unreserved responsibility to the call. It also refers to the redemption of the world toward which Judaism strives.

Relation. *Verhältnis* expresses a relation of proximity or location that does not involve the whole person. It is used to express an *I-It* relation.

Relationship. *Beziehung* refers to a mutual presence, to *I-Thou* relationships that embody a past, a present, and a potential for the future. Relationship refers to a close human bonding in which both partners affirm, accept, and confirm each other.

Speaking. *Gespräch* refers to an open-ended conversation with another that happens on an equal basis between persons without agendas.

Spirit. *Geist* is never a human faculty, or a substance, or any kind of being. "Spirit" exists not inside a person but *between* persons. Humans live in the "spirit" by entering into genuine relationship.

Spirit Becoming Forms. *Geistige Wesenheiten* (translated by Smith and Kaufmann as "Spiritual Beings") refers to that which is perceived *through* a person who then (almost as a vessel) brings what he or she perceives into form. Spirit becoming forms refers to words, creations, and activities resulting from meetings with the *Thou.*

Stand. *Haltung* refers to one's position, stance, or bearing in the world in the presence of a dialogical partner, or nature, or spirit becoming forms.

Turning. *Umkehr* refers to an inner transformation that opens one to enter completely into the presence of the other, without holding back. Turning is the unconditional response of a person to God's call to enter relationship. Turning embodies a double movement: *from* separation and *toward* deep bonding.

Way. *Weg* refers to a unifying life direction that one chooses of turning and going forth to meet the other genuinely and, in the process, to meet the "eternal *Thou.*"

Bibliography

Cited Works by Martin Buber

A Believing Humanism: My Testament, trans. with an Introduction and Explanatory Comments by Maurice Friedman. New York: Simon and Schuster, 1967.
    This book includes Buber's own selections made just before he died of some of the poems and short writings on literature, philosophy, psychology, religion, and social problems that he wished to preserve.

Between Man and Man, trans. Ronald Gregor Smith with an Introduction by Maurice Friedman. New York: Macmillan, 1965.
    This is a book of essays on "Dialogue," "Education," "Education of Character," "The Question to the Single One" (on Kierkegaard), "What Is Man?"—the last a book in itself on philosophical anthropology that lays the groundwork for Buber's mature anthropology *The Knowledge of Man*—and an important Afterword on "The History of the Dialogical Principle." It represents the next stage after *I and Thou* in the development of philosophy of dialogue. Many will find the opening essay "Dialogue" the best introduction to Buber's philosophy.

On the Bible: Eighteen Studies, ed. N. N. Glatzer with an introduction by Herold Bloom. New York: Schocken Books, 1982.
    An important collection of eighteen essays of Buber's on the interpretation of the Bible that supplements his books on the subject.

Daniel: Dialogues on Realization, trans. with an Introductory Essay by Maurice Friedman. New York: Holt, Rinehart, & Winston, 1964.
———
Annotations are from Maurice Friedman's *Encounter on the Narrow Ridge.*

This early book (1913)...is of importance to anyone interested in the development of Buber's thought, his early existentialism, his teaching of holy insecurity and realization, and his approach to drama and poetry. The dialogues are set in the mountains, above the city, in the garden, after the theater, and by the sea and deal with direction, reality, meaning, polarity, and unity.

Eclipse of God: Studies in the Relation Between Religion and Philosophy, **trans. Maurice Friedman and others, with an Introduction by Robert Seltzer. New York: Harper Torchbooks, 1957.**

Eclipse of God is mostly made up of Buber's American lectures in the early 1950s. It is an important statement of philosophy of religion and contains an important critique of the various ways in which such contemporary thinkers as Heidegger, Sartre, Jung, and Bergson have contributed to the eclipse of God by their denial of the reality of transcendence.

Hasidism and Modern Man, **ed. and trans. with an Introduction by Maurice Friedman. Atlantic Highlands, N.J.: Humanities Press International, 1988.**

This is the first of two volumes of Buber's interpretations of Hasidic life and teachings. This volume includes the classic little work *The Way of Man* and "The Life of Hasidism," the famous and beautiful opening of Buber's early *Legend of the Baal-Shem,* as well as "The Baal-Shem-Tov's Instruction in Intercourse with God."

I and Thou, **trans. Ronald Gregor Smith. Edinburgh: T &T Clark, 1937. Second edition, with a Postscript added by the author. New York: Charles Scribner's Sons, 1958. A new translation with a Prologue "I and You" and notes by Walter Kaufmann. New York: Charles Scribner's Sons, 1970.**

I and Thou is Buber's classic work, to which everything written before moves and from which everything written after stems. Ronald Gregor Smith's translation is the best translation, much to be preferred to that of Walter Kaufmann....Kaufmann changes *I-Thou* to I-You, "all real living is meeting" to "all actual life is encounter," and "the turning," to "the return."

Israel and the World: Essays in a Time of Crisis. **New York: Schocken Books, 1963.**

This is an important collection of essays, which for many will be the best introduction to Buber's approach to Judaism. It contains sections on Jewish religiosity, biblical life, learning and education, Israel and the world, and nationalism and Zion.

On Judaism, ed. N. N. Glatzer. New York: Schocken Books, 1972.

On Judaism contains Buber's early "Speeches on Judaism" through which he had an enormous impact on the Jewish youth of Germany and central Europe from 1909 to 1919, influencing many of them to emigrate to Palestine through a combination of an existential-personal approach to Judaism and Zionism. Also published here are the four lectures Buber gave on Judaism in 1951–1952, when he first visited America, the latter originally published as *At the Turning*.

The Knowledge of Man: A Philosophy of the Interhuman, ed. with an Introductory Essay by Maurice Friedman, trans. Maurice Friedman and Ronald Gregor Smith. New York: Harper & Row Publishers, 1965.

This is the mature expression of Buber's philosophical anthropology and as such his most important philosophical statement after *I and Thou*. It explores the distancing and relating that underly the I-Thou and I-It relations and applies this to understanding the interhuman, the common world that we build together through speech-with-meaning, guilt and guilt feelings, the anthropology of art, and "the word that is spoken."

The Letters of Martin Buber, ed. Nahum N. Galatzer. New York: Schocken Books, 1991.

Meetings, ed. and trans. with an Introduction and Bibliography by Maurice Friedman. La Salle, Ill.: Open Court Publishing, 1967.

These are the "Autobiographical Fragments" that Buber wrote or collected for *The Philosophy of Martin Buber* (see the next section).

Moses: The Revelation and the Covenant. Atlantic Highlands, N.J.: Humanities Press International, 1988.

Moses can be regarded as the second of the volumes in Buber's study of the origin of messianism. It is also an important study in itself, and not incidentally, an answer to Freud's *Moses and Monotheism*. There is no natural and supernatural here, but the power of God speaking through the "wonder on the sea."

Pointing the Way: Collected Essays, ed. and trans. with an Introduction by Maurice Friedman. New York: Schocken Books, 1974.

The first, most poetic part of *Pointing the Way* is made up of essays from Buber's beautiful little book *Events and Meetings* (1918), plus

"The Teaching of the Tao." Striking in themselves, these essays are also important in understanding the transition of Buber's thought from his early mysticism to his later philosophy of dialogue.

Tales of the Hasidim: The Early Masters, and *Tales of the Hasidim; The Later Masters,* trans. from the Hebrew by Olga Marx. New York: Schocken Books, 1972.

This is Buber's mature and faithful retelling of what he described as the "legendary anecdotes" of the great Hasidic *zaddikim,* organized according to the rebbes, each with a unique teaching of his own. Even the stories grouped under each rebbe are often subtly interconnected from story to story.

Two Types of Faith, trans. Norman P. Goldhawk. New York: Macmillan, 1986.

This is an impressive and highly controversial study of Jesus and Paul that ranges Jesus with the *emunah,* or unconditional trust in relationship, of the psalmist, the prophets, and Hasidism, Paul with the *pistis* or faith in a knowledge proposition which he shared with John and all those who turned faith into a possession or a gnosis.

The Way of Man: According to the Teachings of Hasidism. New York: Citadel Press, 1995.

Although it takes the form of commentary on Hasidic tales, *The Way of Man* is far more than an interpretation of Hasidism. No one of Buber's works gives us as much of his own simple wisdom as this remarkable distillation.

Buber's Replies to His Critics

Philosophical Interrogations, ed. Sidney and Beatrice Rome. New York: Hope, Rinehart & Winston, 1964.

This book begins with a Buber section conducted and edited and Buber's Responsa translated by Maurice Friedman. The Buber section contains questions by more than thirty philosophers, theologians, and psychotherapists answered by Buber and organized into seven parts: the philosophy of dialogue, theory of knowledge, education, social philosophy, philosophy of religion, the bible and biblical Judaism, and evil. Since the questions and answers are short, it is often more truly dialogical than *The Philosophy of Martin Buber.*

The Philosophy of Martin Buber in **The Library of Living Philosophers,** ed. Paul Arthur Schilpp and Maurice Friedman. La Salle, Ill., and London: Cambridge University Press, 1967.

Actually edited by Maurice Friedman, this book opens with Buber's "Autobiographical Fragments" (published separately as *Meetings*) and closes with Buber's "Replies to Critics," both translated by Maurice Friedman. The fragments are unique of their kind and show how Buber's thought develops as a response to the events and meetings of his life. The Replies, organized under such headings as "philosophical accounting," "I and Thou," theology, mysticism, metaphysics, ethics, the interpretation of the Bible, and Hasidism, contain invaluable material for anyone seriously interested in Buber's philosophy and its applications to many fields.

Cited Books by Maurice Friedman
(in chronological order)

Martin Buber: The Life of Dialogue. London: Routledge & Kegan Paul; Chicago: The University of Chicago Press, 1955.

Professor Buber wrote of it: "To systematize a wild-grown thought such as mine without impairing its elementary character seems to me a remarkable achievement. On a rather multifarious work Dr. Friedman has not imposed an artificial unity; he has disclosed the hidden one. This is the classic study of my thought."

Martin Buber and the Theater, ed. and trans. with three essays by Maurice Friedman. New York: Funk & Wagnalls, 1969.

This book came into being because of Friedman's interest in Buber on drama and that of the editor of Funk & Wagnalls. It includes three essays of Friedman's, in particular Buber's interchange with the great Austrian playwright Hugo von Hofmannsthal concerning the latter's play *The Tower* and the biblical and philosophical background to Buber's "mystery play" *Elijah*.

Touchstones of Reality: Existential Trust and the Community of Peace. New York: E. P. Dutton, 1972.

This little book brings together a lot of Friedman's thoughts on Buber in relation to the philosophy of religion and religion in general.

Bibliography

Martin Buber's Life and Work. 3 volumes: New York: E. P. Dutton, 1981. Paperback edition Detroit, Mich.: Wayne State University Press, 1988.

The first of these three volumes, *The Early Years,* treats Buber's road to *I and Thou,* dealing with his childhood and youth, his mysticism, his philosophy of "realization," the First World War, and the breakthrough to dialogue.

Contemporary Psychology: Revealing and Obscuring the Human. Pittsburgh: Duquesne University Press, 1984.

Contemporary Psychology continues Friedman's concern with the human image, applied specifically to psychology and psychotherapy.

Martin Buber and the Eternal. New York: Human Sciences Press, 1986.

This little book brings together a lot of Friedman's thoughts on Buber in relation to the philosophy of religion and religion in general.

Encounter on the Narrow Ridge: A Life of Martin Buber. New York: Paragon House, 1991.

This book represents an abridgement of Friedman's earlier three volumes of *Martin Buber's Life and Work.* In it, Friedman emphasizes Buber's life more than his works.

Religion and Psychology: A Dialogical Approach. New York: Paragon House, 1992.

Although *Religion and Psychology* touches on subjects that have great relevance for religious psychology, psychology of religion, and pastoral psychology, it is centrally concerned with the *meeting* of religion and psychology and with the issues that grow out of that meeting, such as attitudes toward anxiety, existential trust, the limits of the psyche as touchstone of reality, neurotic and existential guilt, and the limits of the responsibility of the helper.

Other Works Cited

Anderson, Rob, and Kenneth Cissna. 1997. *The Martin Buber–Carl Rogers Dialogue: A New Transcript with Commentary.* New York: State University of New York Press.

Chopra, Deepak. 2001. *How to Know God: The Soul's Journey into the Mystery of Mysteries.* New York: Three Rivers Press.

Eliot, T. S. 1939. *Old Possum's Book of Practical Cats*. New York: Harcourt Brace Jovanovich.

Herman, Jonathan. 1996. *I and Tao: Martin Buber's Encounter with Chuang Tzu*. New York: State University of New York Press.

Horwitz, Rivka. 1988. *Buber's Way to "I and Thou": The Development of Martin Buber's Thought and His "Religion as Presence" Lectures*. Philadelphia: Jewish Publication Society.

Kohanski, Alexander S. 1975. *An Analytical Interpretation of Martin Buber's I and Thou*. New York: Barron's Educational Series.

Mendes-Flohr, Paul. 1989. *From Mysticism to Dialogue: Martin Buber's Transformation of German Social Thought*. Detroit, Mich.: Wayne State University Press.

Merton, Thomas. 1965. *The Way of Chuang Tzu*. New York: New Directions.

Mortensen, C. David. 1997. *Miscommunication*. Thousand Oaks, Calif.: Sage Publications.

Smith, Ronald Gregor. 1967. *Martin Buber*. Richmond, Va.: John Knox Press.

Tannen, Deborah. 1998. *The Argument Culture: Moving from Debate to Dialogue*. New York: Random House.

Vermes, Pamela. 1994. *Buber on God and the Perfect Man*. London: Littman Library of Jewish Civilization.

Wood, Robert E. 1969. *Martin Buber's Ontology: An Analysis of I and Thou*. Evanston, Ill.: Northwestern University Press.

Index

213

Martin Buber's *I and Thou*

Interhuman, 15, 43, 50, 55, 58, 104, 110, 129, 145, 162, 203

Isaac, 131

Jesus, 115–17, 123

Kaufmann, Walter, 10, 11, 17, 22, 25, 38, 43, 49, 81, 102, 104, 108, 140, 142, 153, 155, 158, 177, 183, 192

Kotzk, Rabbi, 149

Landauer, Gustav, 138, 195, 196

Making present, 193, 194, 201

Mendez-Flohr, Paul, 195

Merton, Thomas, 61

Mica, 119, 120

Monologue, 33

Mortensen, C. David, 2, 3

Moses, 131, 141, 142, 144

Mutuality, 22, 24, 48, 81, 104, 123, 184, 185, 191, 198, 204

Mysterium Tremendum, 134, 135, 143, 144, 157

Mysticism, 137–39

Napoleon, 113, 115

Narrow ridge, 78

Nishitani, Keiji, 196, 201

Otto, Rudolf, 134

Obedient listening, 161, 172, 175

Pinhas, Rabbi, 148

Presence, 45, 48, 88, 101, 140, 142, 149, 159, 204

Psychologizing the world, 105

Redemption, 167, 204

Reflexion (bending back on oneself), 158, 165

Rogers, Carl, 138, 175, 189, 190

Rosenzweig, Franz, 98, 142

Scheriftsteller, 4

Shekinah, 88, 148, 149

Smith, Ronald Gregor, 10, 11, 17, 22, 32, 38, 43, 49, 54, 60, 81, 104, 140, 142, 153, 155, 158, 177, 183, 192

Socrates, 113, 114, 122

Spirit, 59, 62, 79, 87, 123, 204

Spirit becoming forms, 7, 50, 60, 63, 65, 205

Tannen, Deborah, 2, 3

Tao, the, 104, 110

Taoism, 110, 122, 139, 150

Trust, 33, 116, 117, 123, 149, 167–69, 175

Turning, 9, 113, 116, 118, 123, 156, 158–65, 168, 170–72, 205

Vermes, Pamela, 110, 169